A Meek and Quiet Spirit

*(Lessons for Wives and Mothers
From Women in the New Testament)*

CINDY HYLES SCHAAP

A Meek and Quiet Spirit

LESSONS FOR
WIVES AND MOTHERS
FROM WOMEN IN THE
NEW TESTAMENT

© Christian Womanhood
8400 Burr Street
Crown Point, Indiana 46307
www.christianwomanhood.org
(219) 365-3202

ISBN 0-9793892-1-6

All Scriptures quotations used in this volume
are taken from the King James Bible.

PAGE LAYOUT AND COVER DESIGN:
Arrow Computer Services, Merrillville, Indiana

OTHER BOOKS BY MRS. CINDY SCHAAP
A Wife's Purpose

Silk and Purple
Lessons for Wives and Mothers
from Women in the Old Testament

Living on the Bright Side
Principles for Lasting Joy, Especially for Ladies

Training Kings and Queens

The Fundamental Man
An Authorized Biography of Jack Frasure Hyles

From the Coal Mines to the Gold Mines
An Authorized Biography of Russell Anderson

Bright Side Planner/Journal

Printed and Bound in the United States of America

Dedication

This book is lovingly dedicated to my only daughter,
Jaclynn April Schaap Weber.

Jaclynn, you are a gift from God,
and He has used your spirit time and time again
to be a great comfort to me.

I love you.

Mom

Table of Contents

Introduction

by Ken and Marlene Schaap

VERY TREASURE HUNTER'S dream is to find a lost treasure chest. The gold prospector's hope is to find the richest vein of gold. The miner searches for the largest and most perfect diamond.

So, every good parent from the time his child is born hopes and prays that one day his son or daughter will find that certain one that God has intended for him. Such was the case with our son Jack. We prayed for years that God would give him that special person in his life to be his wife.

When we first met Cindy, who two years later became Jack's wife, we were standing in the balcony of First Baptist Church in Hammond, Indiana. We saw a group of girls talking in the auditorium. My wife asked Jack, who was a student at Hyles-Anderson College at the time, who the girl with dark hair was. Jack replied, "That is Cindy Hyles."

Whereupon, my wife took Jack's arm and said, "Jack, she is the one; she is the girl we have been waiting for."

After 16 years of marriage, we have seen Cindy become the treasure that Jack was seeking.

In a day when the average woman is more concerned with a career than with a family, Cindy has given herself to being a faithful wife to Jack and a loving and caring mother to her two children, our grandchildren, Jaclynn and Kenny. She is also becoming a well-known and successful writer and author of books.

A Meek and Quiet Spirit

Jesus, in speaking of Mary and Martha, said that Mary had chosen that good part which could not be taken from her. We believe our daughter-in-law has done the same by her life and example to others.

Preface

Without a Word

"Likewise, ye wives, be in subjection to your own husbands; that, if any obey not the word, they also may without the word be won by the conversation of the wives;

While they behold your chaste conversation coupled with fear.

Whose adorning let it not be that outward adorning of plaiting the hair, and of wearing of gold, or of putting on of apparel;

But let it be the hidden man of the heart, in that which is not corruptible, even the ornament of a meek and quiet spirit, which is in the sight of God of great price." (I Peter 3:1-4)

IN I PETER chapter three, wives are told how to change their husbands spiritually. Not only are we told how to see our unsaved husbands become Christians, but we are also told how to help our husbands to correct their spiritual weaknesses. We are told how to help them in the areas where they *"...obey not the word...."*

If these words of instruction work for husbands, I am sure that they can be an enhancement to the training which we, as mothers, give our children also. I Peter 3 is full of instructions for both the wife and the mother, telling what will and **will not** help our loved ones spiritually.

(1) **Our words will not help our husbands spiritually.** Every wife should be aware that words do very little to change a man. Words quickly become nagging, and nagging does more harm than it does good. Because a wife is not given the role of the leader in the home, words of instruction or "preaching" from her lips to her husband's ear are usually inappropriate and even unspiritual. Because of this, God tells us how we can see our husbands change "*without the word.*"

(2) **Our outward appearance will not help our husbands spiritually.** Men enjoy having a beautiful wife. Because a man is stimulated by sight, I believe it is important for a wife to do her best with her physical appearance. However, styling the hair with a lovely hairstyle and wearing beautiful clothes and jewelry will do little to help a man to grow spiritually and to accomplish God's will for his life. The wife who depends upon her outward appearance too much will not be the help meet God intended her to be. She will instead be an unloving and unaffectionate wife and mother who doesn't allow her family to "mess up" her appearance.

(3) **Our chaste conversation will help our family spiritually.** The word *chaste* means *pure from fault; modest or holy.* The word *conversation* means *behavior.* The Bible tells us we can best help our families spiritually not by our words, but by our pure, modest and holy behavior. In others words, our actions speak louder than our words. As Dr. Wendell Evans, the president of Hyles-Anderson College, often says, "Your walk talks, and your talk talks; but your walk talks louder than your talk talks."

I pray each day and ask the Lord to help me to be a good example to my children, and then I strive to be one. For example, I do not teach my children appreciation by nagging them with words. Rather, I strive to teach them appreciation through example. I try to remember to express my gratitude to them for the things that they do for me. Because of expressing my gratitude, I see them learning appreciation.

4 Our *"hidden man of the heart"* or our spirit will help our family spiritually. I must admit that I remember very little about the words spoken by the many Sunday school teachers and Christian school teachers that I had through the years. The teachers I remember most are those whose spirits had something remarkable about them. I remember my favorite Sunday school teacher as having a sincere spirit.

There are two types of spirits which always capture my attention. One is a positive or a rejoicing spirit. My aunt, Mrs. Earlyne Stephens, has influenced me to grow spiritually through her positive spirit. She always has something good to say. She can take something spoken negatively by another and turn it into something positive without even making those around feel awkward. She can find the positive in a negative quality or in a negative person.

Another person who has a positive or a rejoicing spirit is Mrs. Elaine Colsten, the long-time music coordinator at First Baptist Church of Hammond, Indiana. I do not remember many words which have been spoken to me by Mrs. Colsten, though I can say that I remember some. But it is the spirit of Mrs. Colsten which has taught me and helped me the most. How a person can always rejoice is intriguing to me. Mrs. Colsten's spirit is an unsolved mystery to me. Her spirit draws my attention to her, making me want to learn from her and be like her.

I once heard an evangelist's wife say that she cried every time she took her husband to the airport. Needless to say, her husband dreaded each trip and his time with her. One day, after giving her husband to the Lord, she quit crying on the way to the airport. She learned instead to talk positively to her husband, and this change in her spirit mystified her husband. She said that he stared wonderingly at her all the way from then on.

I call this *mystique*. I am mystified by the spirit of someone who is always positive, and I am more attracted to this type of person.

The second type of spirit which helps me to grow spiritually is a consistent spirit. My aunt and Mrs. Colsten are not only positive and rejoicing in their spirits, but they are *always* positive and rejoicing. Again, there is something magnetic about a consistent spirit. It draws my attention to the people who possesses it and causes me to want to investigate their lives and learn from them.

The Bible also tells us of two types of spirits which will help others to grow spiritually.

⑤ A meek spirit will help our family spiritually. This word *meek* in I Peter chapter three means *gentle* or *of a soothing disposition.* In other words, our gentleness can make our husbands great.

In Psalm 18:35b the Bible says, *"...Thy gentleness hath made me great."* Jesus' patience with me when I am wrong and His love and care for me when I am in need has helped me to grow as a Christian.

My patience with my family, especially when they are wrong, and my concern for meeting their needs, especially when they are discouraged, is my best tool in helping them spiritually.

Let me ask you, "How gentle are you when your husband has made a mistake?" Do you yell or scream at him? Do you slam doors or kitchen cabinets? That doesn't sound very gentle to me!

Do you try to contain your disappointment in your husband with as much patience as you can muster? Do you regard his feelings as more important than any embarrassment or inconvenience his mistakes might have cost you?

How gentle are you when your child is hurting? Do you say, "Don't bother me; I'm busy"? Are you hasty and harsh in your words and actions when a skinned knee or some other burden is brought to your attention? Do you slow down so that you might cleanse the wound without causing your child more pain? Do you aid him in his sorrow with both attention and affection?

Are you gentle? If not, you are missing a wonderful opportunity to change your family spiritually.

The word *meek* in the Bible also means *even.* If a wife is meek, she sees all people as her equals, her family included. She does not see herself as being superior to her children, nor does she see herself as being inferior to her husband. Because of this, she does not need to demand her rights. Rather, she can be a servant. She can rule her children with gentleness, and she can obey her husband with confidence.

⑥ A quiet spirit will help our family spiritually. The word *quiet* in I Peter chapter three means *tranquillity arising from within, causing no disturbance to others.* A positive or a rejoicing spirit comes from having a peace or a tranquillity within. Mrs. Elaine Colsten is often teased about talking a lot. She is an outgoing person, whereas I am more shy. But Mrs. Colsten possesses what the Bible calls a quiet spirit because she is always the same. She has a peace which comes from her *"hidden man of the heart."*

Again, there is something about a person who is always calm and always at peace which attracts the attention of others. Let me ask you, "Are you always calm and at peace when your husband and your children arrive home?" or "Do they wonder what kind of mood you will possess?" The world would tell you that constant change keeps a person interesting. The Bible tells us just the opposite! It is our own personal walk with the Lord which gives us the ability to be at peace and to be consistent.

The word *quiet* also means "causing no disturbance to others." Having a quiet spirit does not mean never talking above a whisper; nor does it mean never having a laughing good time. It does mean, however, that we are not a disturbance to others. When we walk into a room, we are not so loud that we interrupt conversations and make it difficult for people to continue their work. We are not constantly disturbing others by drawing attention to ourselves.

Sometimes people who are very quiet in their volume are very loud and bold in their spirits by saying such things as this:

- "I have my rights!"

- "Nobody appreciates me."

- "I wish someone would notice all the work that I do."

A Meek and Quiet Spirit

I have entitled my book on New Testament women, *A Meek and Quiet Spirit* because that is the description for wives and mothers in the New Testament which stands out in my mind.

My dad has said that he believes the *"hidden man of the heart"* referred to in I Peter 3:4 is really the man whom God has made a particular woman to complete. The hidden man of my heart is Dr. Jack Schaap. Since the day I married my husband, helping him has been the utmost desire which I have carried in my heart. I believe with all of my heart that my purpose in life is to help him to do what God would have him to do.

The Bible says that I can do this without saying a word. In fact, saying nothing is usually the best policy. I can help my husband spiritually by possessing a meek and quiet spirit.

My prayer is that this book will improve the spirits of the wives and mothers who read its pages. I desire all of our spirits to be more meek, to be quieter, after having read the Bible stories and the lessons therein. This book is not mainly to help us to help ourselves. Rather, it is to help us to help others spiritually, particularly our husbands. Please help me to accomplish this or I have failed.

Thank you for sharing another book with me.

Cindy Schaap
I Samuel 12:24

Being Used of the Lord in a Special Way

A Lesson From Mary

"Therefore the Lord himself shall give you a sign;
Behold, a virgin shall conceive,
and bear a son, and shall call his name Immanuel."
(Isaiah 7:14)

Chapter 1
Mary
Luke 1:26-56

*T*HERE ISN'T A woman alive who really loves the Lord who does not wish to be used of the Lord as Mary was. I am one of those women. Because I have grown up as a prosperous American citizen, I not only have grown up with a desire to serve the Lord, but I have also felt the flame of a desire to be successful. Success is a part of our American dream, and it is a drive which lies within me.

When I think of being used of the Lord in a special way, what better example could come to my mind than the example of Mary? Yet when I study her life on this earth, I find that her being used of the Lord did not necessarily coincide with what we American ladies would call success. However, through the eyes of eternity, Mary's life surely qualifies as one of the most successful. I would like to begin this book by analyzing the life of Mary and by discovering what her life can teach us about what is truly spiritual success.

(1) **Purity brings spiritual success.** I have a pastor friend who used to be a performer in Nashville before his salvation. During his career, his path crossed with many elite Hollywood movie stars. He has shared with others the wicked living he witnessed firsthand among the "successful" in Hollywood. Many of the women who become famous actresses, he says, receive their opportunities by participating in immoral relationships with certain directors and producers. Impurity is often a tool which is used to obtain worldly success.

Spiritual success requires just the opposite. The young girl God chose to mother Jesus was a pure girl who had not known her fiancé or any other man in a physical way. The Bible says in Isaiah 7:14, *"Therefore the Lord himself shall give you a sign; Behold, a virgin shall conceive, and bear a son, and shall call his name Immanuel."*

Though God forgives and uses the Rahabs of the Bible, when it came time for God to choose a mother for His Son, God chose someone who was pure. (Rahab was the harlot who later became a Christian and was a part of the genealogy of Jesus Christ.) Any woman would esteem it a sacred honor to mother the Saviour, but not many women are willing to live with the purity which Mary did.

Sometimes we may even ask ourselves, "What's the use of living pure, when so many do not, yet are still accepted and used in the church?" After all, God does forgive, and He will use us anyway. Yes, God will forgive and use the Rahabs of this world, but it takes a completely pure vessel to be a Mary.

$\textcircled{2}$ **Humility brings spiritual success.** The drawback of living a pure life is that it brings a temptation toward pride. Many a pure Christian woman has a difficult time not disdaining the woman whose past is tainted by sin. We do not find this spirit, however, in the life of Mary. In Luke 1:38, Mary calls herself a handmaid (or a servant) of the Lord. *"And Mary said, Behold the handmaid of the Lord; be it unto me according to thy word...."* (Luke 1:38)

Mary then submissively invited the Lord to have His way in her life. In our looking back several generations later, it may seem quite easy for Mary to have responded to the angel of the Lord in that way. However, it had to have been very tough at the time. I believe that while Mary must have been a very humble lady, she also must have been a very tough lady.

It took both humility and strength for Mary to tell her fiancé that she was with child of the Holy Ghost. Joseph could have had Mary killed for being found with child had he thought the child was from another man. Mary's excellent and godly choice of a husband was a help to her at this time. The wrong husband is definitely a hindrance in being used of the Lord. Though Joseph had enough faith in God to believe that this child was indeed conceived from the Holy Spirit, Mary still had to bear the shame and reproach of "what the neighbors would think." We would think that spiritual success surely brings with it a good reputation, but this is not necessarily the case.

It took both humility and strength to bring forth a child in a barn and in poverty. Luke 2:7 tells us, *"And she brought forth her firstborn son, and wrapped him in swaddling clothes, and laid him in a manger; because there was no room for them in the inn."*

We, as American ladies, tend to feel that we need to have an adequately decorated and prepared nursery and a comfortable birthing room in a hospital in order to have a completely "natural" childbirth. How God must laugh at our ideas! Mary's experience was the epitome of truly natural childbirth. And while there is nothing wrong with beginning a child's life both safely and properly, it amuses me how little we know about what is natural.

Not only do we deem a prosperous start to be essential in becoming a successful mother, but we also feel that we must put away for our children's college education so that they might give **their** children an even better advantage. Again, this is not wrong, but it is a far cry from being a qualification for the spiritually successful. Mary's Son, Jesus Christ, **chose** poverty as His way of birth and also as His way of life.

It also took humility and strength for Mary to start her child's life on the run as she did. She did not give birth to Jesus in a sanitized hospital room, and she did not bring Him home to a lovely nursery to be coddled by family and friends. Instead, she fled with her husband to Egypt, because Joseph had been told by an angel that Herod was seeking to kill Jesus. *"And when they were departed, behold, the angel of the Lord appeareth to Joseph in a dream, saying, Arise, and take the young child and his mother, and flee into Egypt, and be thou there until I bring thee word: for Herod will seek the young child to destroy him."* (Matthew 2:13)

Surely Mary's faith in God and His plan was tested at this time, which leads me to the third qualification for obtaining spiritual success.

(3) **Faith brings spiritual success.** Luke 2:19 is one of my favorite verses in the Bible. *"But Mary kept all these things, and pondered them in her heart."* God used the angels and the spiritual Christians with whom Mary came in contact (such as the shepherds) to assure her that her Son was going to be used of God in a special way. Her mission was to rear the Saviour. As Mary experienced with her Son what humanly would seem to be failure after failure in His life and misunderstanding after misunderstanding, Mary meditated upon the promises she had received from God. It was her faith in those promises that allowed her to stay true to Jesus even when she could not understand the life of her own Son. Mary did not broadcast these promises, however. She kept them in her heart, making it difficult, I'm sure, for her to be understood by even those closest to her. Mary had enough faith, however, to believe that God could indeed use her, just as she was, not because of her, but because of God's greatness.

(4) **Sacrifice brings spiritual success.** I believe that Mary's first taste of letting go of Jesus took place when Jesus was twelve years old. Mary and Joseph had gone with Jesus to Jerusalem to celebrate the Passover. When it was time for them to return home, both mother and father were surprised to see that Jesus was not with them. They found Jesus three days later in the temple hearing and asking questions. Understandably, Mary and Joseph were a bit frustrated after their long search for their Son. Jesus responded to their frustration by saying, *"…How is it that ye sought me? wist ye not that I must be about my Father's business?"*

The Bible tells us in Luke 2:50, and 51 that they could not understand what Jesus said to them at that time, but Mary kept these sayings in her heart. She pondered what Jesus had said to her though she did not fully understand. And I believe a light was dawning in her soul that spiritual success is not about gaining, but it is more about letting go and losing what is most precious to you.

Spiritual motherhood is not about placing your children under your thumb so that they will be sure to bring their parents joy in their old age. Rather it is letting go so that those children might become not what we deem to be successful, but rather what God deems to be successful.

In Mark 3:31-35, Mary seems to have used her relationship with Jesus to gain His attention from the crowd. Jesus reminded His disciples that His mother and His brethren were not truly His family. Mary was reminded as she called for Jesus that it was her responsibility to share her Son with all those who would do His will and would minister with Him.

Again, Mary was reminded in John 2:4 at the marriage at Cana that her Son needed her to let go of mothering Him in order that He might do something greater. Mary responded with obedience by replying to the servants around her, "...whatsoever he saith unto you, do it." What a sacrifice it was for Mary to share her Son with so many people.

Yet the greatest sacrifice must have been contained in Jesus' crucifixion. I'm sure Mary must have known the Old Testament, and she must have been aware of what was to be her Son's final fate. Surely it was with difficulty that she looked toward the future as she cuddled the tiny form of her precious child.

How great must have been her pain when she heard the criticism and the persecution her Son endured during His simple and short earthly ministry. How heartbreaking must have been those days of His being tried, convicted and finally crucified on a cross at the young age of 33 years. Humanly speaking, the life of Mary's son was not something about which a mother could boast. It would not be like rearing a doctor or the President of the United States. It was not even like rearing a famous preacher for God. Humanly speaking, it was so much less...but spiritually speaking it was so much more.

Mary stood true to the end. She was there with Jesus until His death, having never forsaken Him. And her Son did accomplish what He set out to do. He is the Saviour of the world.

I do not wish to deify Mary as the Catholics do. The Bible obviously teaches us that Mary was human, and she was a sinner who also needed a Saviour. It records to us times when Mary was afraid and frustrated. But I do want to brag on Mary for her spiritual success. I don't think any other woman has been more spiritually successful than Mary.

Because Mary is human and not deity, I don't think the Lord will mind if I finish this chapter by comparing Mary to myself and to you, my readers. Allow me to do so by sharing these points with you:

A. *We, like Mary, are on a mission.* I have a husband, Jack Schaap, who is called of God to be a preacher. At this writing, I have a 15-year-old daughter, Jaclynn, who has surrendered to full-time Christian work. I have an 11-year-old son Kenny who believes he has been called to preach. My mission is to be sure that I do my part to help my husband and children to fulfill whatever it is that God has for them to do. I am as convinced of this being my mission as I am convinced that Jesus did indeed die for me on the cross.

B. *We, like Mary, must remain humble as we seek to accomplish our mission.* As I seek to be what my husband and children would need, I find that my days are filled with many humble tasks. I am a teacher and a writer, but I find that I spend more time doing mundane tasks—the tasks of a simple handmaid—so that my husband would be free to accomplish his work for the Lord. I find that the things which God calls upon me to do in order to build a relationship with my children are often humble and seemingly insignificant tasks. I find that seeking poverty rather than riches is a necessary part of my role in guiding my children toward seeking the kingdom of God rather than the world. The world would not esteem my lot in life as that of a successful one. Neither would some Christians who do not understand my mission.

C. *We, like Mary, must have faith in order to carry out our mission.* I have my days when I hear the world's cry. I hear the cry of the success-oriented liberated women of American culture. And I wonder if I am wasting my life by giving so much to so few. It is then that I remember the promises of God. He has given me some personal promises, not by way of angels or shepherds or wise men, but by way of many quiet times in His Word in the early morning hours. I ponder in my heart the promises from my Saviour, and I have renewed faith to invest in my mission, no matter what it takes.

D. *We, like Mary, must be willing to sacrifice in order to fulfill our mission.* As a pastor's daughter, I have found my greatest difficulty to be in sharing my parents with those who work with them. I have been reminded time and time again by the Lord that this is **my** cross, as it was Mary's—a small cross, perhaps, but a heavy one for me sometimes. I must share my parents and now also my preacher-husband with those to whom God has called them. I cannot cling to them nor claim them as my own. Someday I must do the same with my children. I must invest in them only to lose them to their life's mates and to the people to whom God has called them to minister. And I must realize that the task for which God is preparing them may not be a task which will necessarily reap great benefits in this world.

Mary was proclaimed by an angel to be the mother of our Saviour. What a great moment that must have been! The Bible tells us that Mary rejoiced and praised the Lord at this time! But from there she descended. She became less and less "successful" until finally her Son did what He set out to do. He died in shame and disgrace. Centuries later, however, we realize her to be the most spiritually successful of all women. Oh, to learn from Mary rather than from the world what it truly means to be spiritually successful! Oh, to be used of the Lord in a special way.

*"Lord, make me willing to **descend** to what,
in Your eyes, is indeed spiritual success."*

Making Room for Others

A Lesson From Elisabeth

*"But the angel said unto him, Fear not, Zacharias:
for thy prayer is heard;
and thy wife Elisabeth shall bear thee a son,
and thou shalt call his name John."*
(Luke 1:13)

Chapter 2
Elisabeth
Luke 1:5-80

"THE PREACHER'S KIDS are usually the worst kids in the church." This is a statement which I have heard a few times and to which I have always cringed a bit. Because I am both a preacher's "kid" and a preacher's wife (which has made me the mother of preacher's "kids"), I find the stigma which accompanies the position a bit distasteful.

I am thankful for Elisabeth's life because it "shoots" this stigma full of holes. Elisabeth, like myself, was a preacher's kid. The Bible says that she was "...*of the daughters of Aaron....*" (Luke 1:5) Aaron was the high priest under Moses' leadership.

Elisabeth was also the wife of a preacher. Her husband was the priest Zacharias. In Luke 1:6, God gives this description of this preacher's "kid" and her husband: "*And they were both righteous before God, walking in all the commandments and ordinances of the Lord blameless.*" I surely desire this verse to describe my life, even though I am a bratty preacher's "kid."

Zacharias and Elisabeth could have thought they had reason to disobey the Lord and to become bitter. For after many years of marriage, they had remained childless. Yet God describes their lives as being blameless before Him.

When Elisabeth was older, an angel of the Lord appeared to her husband and told him that Elisabeth was going to bear a son and that she was to call her son "*John.*" Because of lack of faith, Zacharias was smitten with dumbness of speech which lasted until the birth of John.

MAKING ROOM FOR OTHERS

God did bless Zacharias and Elisabeth with a son, and they obeyed God by naming him John. People wondered why they used this particular name. It was custom in those days for a child to be named after a member of the family. But this couple showed their obedience to the Lord by naming their son John and by not being concerned about the thoughts of others.

What I love best about Elisabeth, though, is the humility she displayed toward her cousin Mary. Mary came to share with Elisabeth that she was to become the mother of the Messiah. Surely Mary, as a young girl, had some doubts about the reality of the vision she and Joseph shared. Perhaps that is why she fled to her elder cousin with her news. Perhaps she felt she could trust the righteous Elisabeth to help to increase her faith not only in God, but also in herself and in her ability to rear the Son of God.

Put yourself in Elisabeth's shoes for a while. While still carrying her own promised son, a much younger Mary, her own cousin, comes to her and proclaims herself to be the mother of the Messiah. Imagine what Elisabeth's reactions could have been:

"Mary, you're too young to be used of the Lord in that way!"

"Mary, who do you think you are coming to me with news like that? I don't believe it—I am of the daughters of Aaron and not you!"

"Why you're not even married to a preacher like I am!"

Imagine what Elisabeth could have thought: "Why would the Lord choose my younger cousin and not me?"

Occasionally, in my travels I am confronted with pastors' wives who are jealous of the assistant pastor's wife or vice versa. And I think to myself, "It's a good thing one of these ladies is not Mary's cousin. There just wouldn't be room for a Mary in their lives." Not that I blame them a bit. I often tell my children to remember that there is always room for others in the Lord's work. One need not feel envious of the way that the Lord uses others. And when I remind my children of this, I realize that I am often just "preaching" a much-needed sermon to myself.

A Meek and Quiet Spirit

I believe that the greatest work that Elisabeth did prior to rearing John the Baptist was to confirm the faith of little Mary, the young spiritual giant, who was to give birth to Jesus. In Luke 1:42 and 43, Elisabeth's humble reaction is found: *"...Blessed art thou among women, and blessed is the fruit of thy womb. And whence is this to me, that the mother of my Lord should come to me?"*

I wonder if you or I would be too proud to call a young person or a peer *"the mother of my Lord"* had we been in Elisabeth's shoes. Yet Elisabeth expressed with humility that she did not even feel worthy to be in her young cousin's presence. Luke 1:44 and 45 say, *"For, lo, as soon as the voice of thy salutation sounded in mine ears, the babe leaped in my womb for joy. And blessed is she that believed: for there shall be a performance of those things which were told her from the Lord."*

The Bible tells us that baby John jumped in Elisabeth's womb as soon as he heard Mary's news. Every mother remembers how exciting the first kick in the womb is. I believe that God caused baby John to have his first kick at this time, and what a kick it seems to have been! After Elisabeth perceived what was happening in her womb, she confirmed Mary's faith by saying something like this: "Mary, I'm so glad that you have believed the Lord in this matter; I believe it, too!" Elisabeth encouraged Mary's heart by telling her that the things she was believing would surely come to pass.

I would love to be an encourager of people like Elisabeth was. But in order to be such an encourager, I must swallow some pride and have a spirit of humility. In order to be a confirmer of another's faith, I must be willing to make room for others, even if I sometimes seem to be crowded out.

In reflecting on the life of Elisabeth, I have been reminded by the Holy Spirit of those who have made room for me. I am almost afraid to mention any names because I may leave out someone who is very important to me. But I must mention a few.

I must begin with my mom and dad. I have often thought of how difficult it must be to read the writings and to hear the teachings of your own daughter. While I know there is a sense of pride in the accomplishments of one's own child, there is also the realization of the weaknesses of that child. Who knows a child's faults more than her own parents? Though my parents are older and much more experienced than I, they have always encouraged me in my writing and in my teaching. My mother has even graciously sought my advice a time or two, something I am sure I needed more than she.

The first time I spoke in a conference with my mother, I went straight to my motel room when I was finished. I fell on my knees and cried. I did not want to appear as smart as my mother in any way. I wanted her to feel honored, and I did not wish to take from that honor. Yet many times God has used my mother to be my greatest cheerleader.

I think of my in-laws who know that I am not a perfect wife or mother. Yet the biggest promoters of my books on marriage have been my in-laws. If I could hire them as full-time salesmen, I surely would never want for anything again. I am aware that these wonderful people are simply making room for their daughter-in-law.

I think of friends like Jane Grafton, Pam Wallace, Linda Stubblefield, and Carol Frye Tudor. There are too many friends to mention. But these four names stand out as the names of friends who have confirmed my faith in myself and who have made room for me. All of them are very talented and busy women. Yet, it seems I never cross their paths without hearing their words of kindness and praise and without having my faith confirmed.

Jane and Carol are two of my favorite speakers and authors. How precious to me that they are also the two people who most praise my own speaking and writing. Without Linda Stubblefield's having made room for me in her busy schedule, there would positively be no books written by Cindy Schaap. Linda truly possesses the spirit of Elisabeth. (And she's not even a preacher's kid—Humph!) And Pam Wallace is one of those friends with whom I believe I could share my greatest victory and from whom I would receive nothing but support.

The Bible clearly gives us the reason why these women are the way they are. In Luke 1:41 we read that Elisabeth was filled with the Holy Ghost. Why are so many women unable to make room for other women? Because in order to confirm the faith of others, a woman must be filled with the Holy Spirit. She must be building a relationship with the Bible and in prayer so that she can possess the spirit of humility which Elisabeth had.

It was very necessary for Elisabeth to possess this spirit because she was not to rear the Son of God. Instead she was to rear the great and, yet, humble John the Baptist who would point others to Jesus. She reared a son who said, "*...but he that cometh after me is mightier than I, whose shoes I am not worthy to bear....*" (Matthew 3:11b) John also said, "*He must increase, but I must decrease.*" (John 3:30) Could it be that John learned this humble spirit from his mother? I think so! Would he have been the humble servant who preached repentance in the wilderness while dressed in camel's hair and eating locusts and wild honey had his mother had a spirit of pride? I think not!

Perhaps God is preparing you to do some great work for Him? Perhaps God is preparing you to encourage another who will do some great work for Him. Perhaps God's plan is for you to live, dress, and eat in luxury. Perhaps He is preparing you to minister to some who do, while you do not. Perhaps God is preparing you to rear a child whose name will be known in the annals of Christian history. Perhaps God is preparing you to rear a child who will encourage another's child to do a great work. Whatever God is calling you to do, He will use you in a great way (not necessarily in a big way) if you are humble enough to do His will, whatever it may be.

My prayer for you and for me is that the Lord would grant to us a spirit of humility so that we can be prepared to do whatever it is that God has made us to do. I pray that we all would be willing to make room for others, as others have so humbly made room for us. Perhaps it would help if we would keep before us the knowledge of where we would be, had God not provided a way to make room for us.

Complete Healing

A Lesson From the Woman With the Issue of Blood

"And Jesus said, Somebody hath touched me:
for I perceive that virtue is gone out of me."
(Luke 8:46)

Chapter 3
The Woman with the Issue of Blood
Matthew 9:18-26

A WOMAN HAD BEEN sick for 12 years with a physically draining disease. She had seen many doctors about her disease, and according to the Scripture, these doctors had put her through an awful lot. She had spent all of her money trying to find a cure, and in spite of it all, she only grew worse.

This woman had heard of a man named Jesus Who could heal the sick and even raise the dead. She sought Jesus and found Him on His way to the home of the ruler Jairus, whose daughter had just died. A great throng followed Jesus to see what Jesus would do about this dead girl. It was very difficult for the woman to get to Jesus because of the crowd.

I believe this woman must have known God, and she must have been waiting for the Messiah for a long time. It was not difficult for her to believe that Jesus was the Son of God and that He could heal her. She felt that even if she could just touch the hem of Jesus' garment, she would be healed. That is exactly what the woman did! As soon as she touched Jesus, her fountain of blood was dried up and *"...she felt in her body that she was healed...."* (Mark 5:29b) How wonderful that after all the drain of this disease, after all of the visits to doctors, after all the money spent, and after twelve long years, this woman received complete physical healing.

However, I think that there was something more to the healing that this woman received. For Jesus turned about and in Luke 8:45 questioned, *"...Who touched me?..."* His disciples thought it strange that Jesus would want to know who touched His clothes, seeing that there were so many people near. Any one of them could have accidentally brushed against His clothes any number of times. But Jesus perceived that virtue had gone out of Him. *Virtue* is defined as *the quality of moral righteousness or excellence; any admirable quality or trait; purity.* Because of these definitions, I believe that this woman was healed spiritually as well as being healed physically.

The woman had considerable respect for Jesus. Realizing that she was the one who had been the recipient of His virtue, she fell down at Jesus' feet and told Him all about what had happened. Jesus told the woman that it was her faith in Him which had healed her, and He sent her away healed and in peace.

In this story there are lessons to be learned, not only to the physically ill, but also to the spiritually ill. Every reader, I'm sure, has some need of spiritual healing. I know in my own life I have come to Jesus begging to be delivered from some besetting sins. Though I have not yet arrived, there are some sins from which I have been miraculously healed.

Fear is one example of such a sin. I prayed for a long time that God would heal me from the sin of fear. I had an abnormal fear of being alone and other things which greatly hindered my spiritual life. The steps I took to be healed of fear greatly parallel with the steps this woman took to be healed. Allow me to share them with you.

1 **I fought the crowd to get to Jesus.** The Bible seems to be teaching us in this story that not everyone who walks with Jesus receives virtue from Him. There are many Christians who faithfully attend church and who spend a little bit of time with the Lord on a pretty consistent basis; however, they do not really touch Jesus. The crowd of those who call upon Jesus' name once a week when they attend church or when they are in a jam would be numerous. Very few are the people who really get through this great throng of mediocre Christians to really touch Jesus.

(2) **I touched Jesus through daily Bible reading and prayer.** Just to read a few verses on a fairly consistent schedule is not enough. The Christian who really seeks healing, whether physical or spiritual, needs to have a lengthy quiet time at least once a day where he seeks the Lord with his whole heart. It is this daily quiet time which reveals to us our sin and our need to be healed from it. As we get closer to becoming totally dependent on our relationship with the Lord, we can be healed from our sin.

(3) **I believed that God would deliver me from my sin.** The closer I get to Jesus, the more I understand that I must not ask just for healing. I must believe in His ability to heal me, and I must express that belief to Christ. I must not tell myself that I am just a _____ person (you fill in the blank) and cannot have victory over my lifetime habits. I must keep touching the Lord daily, knowing that He will heal.

(4) **I feared God's judgment upon my sin.** The woman with the issue of blood fell down before Jesus fearing and trembling when He asked, "...*Who touched me?...*" One reason we do not receive or seek healing from our sin is that we are comfortable with our pet sins such as fear, pride, jealousy, etc. We do not fear God's wrath upon the "small" sins in our lives. We do not realize the blessings that we miss because we harbor these sins in our lives. We must fear God, and we must fear breaking any of His commandments so that we may truly see healing in our lives.

(5) **I was honest with Jesus.** Honesty, I believe, has been a very important ingredient in my Christian life. I have always told God with what sins I am struggling. If someone has hurt my feelings, if I feel jealous or angry with someone, I tell God. If I feel cold and apathetic in my spiritual life or in my soul winning, I tell God. There is no real virtue in telling God all about it because He knows anyway. Yet many Christians cannot communicate with God because they do not feel the freedom to tell God their feelings. Many Christians are trying to hide something from God. Great Christians who have fallen into deep sin will tell you that dishonesty with God was the beginning of their long slide. Christians who have come back to God from deep sin will tell you that their honesty with God began their long climb back. The woman in this story told Jesus all the truth. I want to tell Jesus all the truth also.

6 **I was ashamed of my sin.** We must see our pet sin such as pride as heinous a sin as the debilitating disease with which this woman suffered. We must be as sick of our pet sin as this woman was of her sickness. We must be as desperate for healing as this woman was.

7 **I realized that all of my human efforts would only make my spiritual condition worse.** Many people never rise above their besetting sins because they keep deciding to **try** to be a better Christian. It was a wonderful day in my life when I realized that the Christian life was not about my trying to live right. The Christian life is about my seeking and touching Jesus. He does the healing as I draw close to Him. Until I draw close to Him and stay close to Him, all of my efforts to overcome sin will be in vain.

This story can be paralleled to salvation. This woman had gone to doctors for 12 years and had spent all of her money seeking a cure. Many people today go to many different religions and doctors (priests) seeking a cure from their sin. They give their money to these "priests" and still struggle on their way to Hell. If they would fall at Jesus' feet and tell Him the whole truth about their sinful condition, their faith would save them from their sin.

8 **I believed that Jesus would take note of me amidst the crowd.** I often remind myself of Jesus' love and forgiveness as I seek His face. This helps me to believe that He will hear my prayers for spiritual healing even as many others call upon Him for help.

After you have followed the above-mentioned steps, three things will take place in your life.

A. *You will receive virtue from Christ.* The closer I get to Jesus, the more I feel His righteousness filling my life. If I decide to ignore Jesus for just one day, however, I see that the virtue in my life is not my own. It is Jesus' virtue. It is not me who has changed. I am the same sinner I was before. It is Christ in me Who makes the change.

B. *You will receive peace from Christ.* God sent the woman away in peace—a state of tranquillity. Each touch I have ever received from Jesus has left me in a state of peacefulness.

C. *You will receive* **complete** *spiritual healing.* It may seem sometimes that we must wait a long time for God to heal us from our besetting sins. Yet when Jesus does heal us, His healing is complete. I prayed for years that God would heal me from my fear. One day I realized that the fear was gone. I cannot tell you when it left. I cannot tell you of any methods I used to "overcome" my fear. God simply answered my prayer, and I was completely healed. I touched Jesus, and His virtue of faith replaced my fear. I am not saying that I have never been afraid since that day, but fear has not had its hold on me since that day. Whenever I have felt fear since, I have simply taken hold once more to the hem of Jesus' garment, and the fear has left. I have been spiritually healed—completely healed. I now have more sins from which I need deliverance, but I believe that someday they will have no hold on me.

Do you know why the woman with the issue of blood went to Jesus for healing? She went because she had heard of Him. Someone had cared enough to tell her about Jesus and His ability to heal. How sweet to have a God Whom I can touch and Who can touch me. How sweet is the deliverance from Hell and from sin in my Christian life. How selfish to keep it to myself. I must tell others through soul winning. I must tell my children, my friends, my neighbors that Jesus can heal them. Sin does not have to keep its hold on them. There is no sin which they cannot overcome. Praise the Lord! We must tell them.

Give It Back to God

A Lesson From Peter's Mother-in-Law

"My son, attend to my words;
incline thine ear unto my sayings.
For they are life unto those that find them,
and health to all their flesh."
(Proverbs 4:20, 22)

Chapter 4
Peter's Mother-in-Law
Matthew 8:14, 15; Mark 1:29-31;
Luke 4:38, 39

*I*N THESE VERSES we have another account of Jesus' healing sickness. Jesus had just left the synagogue, and He entered into Peter's house. When Jesus arrived, some people sought Him to tell Him that Peter's mother-in-law lay sick of a fever. The Bible says that Jesus touched her hand, and her fever left her. Then the Bible tells us that she immediately rose and ministered unto them.

As stated in a previous chapter, when Jesus heals, He certainly does heal completely. His healing was so complete that Peter's mother-in-law was immediately able to minister to Jesus and to the others who were with Him. This word *minister* in this passage means *to wait on as a guest* or *to serve at a table*. So Peter's mother-in-law took her newfound strength and used it for the Lord and others.

I believe that this story basically defines what the ministry is. Allow me to share that definition with you.

(1) **Christian ministry is taking what God has done in your life and sharing it with others.** This is what I have done in my life. God has taught me some wonderful things, and He has done some marvelous things in my life. I constantly try to share with others what He has done for me. Not only do I share what God has done for me throughout my life, but I am also careful to keep learning and growing so that I always have something fresh to share with others. I want

to share what God has done in my life LATELY.

My dad often explained the verse John 8:32 which says, *"And ye shall know the truth, and the truth shall make you free."* Once we learn a truth from God's Word, we are free to learn another truth. It is the sharing of the truth which we have learned which often frees us to learn another truth. Let me ask you, "What has God done in your life lately? How are you sharing it with others?" If you feel God hasn't done anything in your life lately, you need to follow the steps prescribed in chapter 11 about Mary Magdalene so that God can indeed work in your life.

(2) Christian ministry is taking what God has given you and sharing it with others. What resources has God given you? Are you sharing them with others? Perhaps God has given you an extra amount of money or material goods. Are you sharing them with others? Even those who are poor in worldly goods should share a portion of what they have with others.

What abilities has God given you? Are you sharing them with others? This is what I have done with my life. I have taken whatever abilities God has given me and shared them with others in whatever way I could. In the process, God has given me some more abilities. He has also improved my self-esteem. In using my own God-given abilities, I have been free to quit comparing myself with other women, and I have been able to find my worth in God's unique purpose for my life.

(3) Christian ministry is sharing what God has given you and done for you with your family. My family would tell you that I am very free to share with them what God has done in my life. In the last few weeks, the Lord has really been dealing in my heart in the area of complaining. I recently shared with my daughter how I felt God working in this area and how I had seen some improvement. God is touching me and healing me in this area, and I immediately want to share what God has done for me, not only with my friends and acquaintances, but also with my family.

Sometimes, it takes humility to share your spiritual sicknesses with others so that you might share with them how God has healed you. But this type of testimony teaching is most effective. When sharing what God has done, we should prayerfully consider first what should be said. Yes, there are some personal mistakes in our lives which are better left unsaid. But the best kind of parenting and the best kind of teaching, I believe, come from candid teaching. That is sharing with our family and with others how God has healed us lately.

I want to be sure that I use what abilities God has given me for my family also. I want to use my writing not only to bless the people who buy my books, many of whom are strangers. I especially want to use my writing abilities to warm the hearts of my family through kind letters to them.

Many a husband struggles with the fact that his wife is so busy using her abilities for the church and for different organizations that she has little time to use them at home for her family. I am definitely not against using your abilities outside the home. But the Christian wife's first priority is to use them inside the home. I want to use my "way with words" to help me to encourage my husband. I don't wish to be an accomplished writer and speaker who is a witch with her words at home. I want to use my domestic abilities to bless others. But for every time I bake to encourage someone else, I need to bake to encourage those who live in my home.

④ **Most of all, Christian ministry is using what God has done for you to minister to Him.** I am so glad that my pastor has taught me to minister to God. We are taught so often to take our burdens to God and to bring requests to Him that we sometimes forget why we were made. We were not made to get our prayers answered. God did not make Adam in the Garden of Eden so that he could get his prayers answered. God made Adam to fellowship with God.

Yes, God wants to minister to us, but He also wants us to minister to Him. Again, let me ask you, "What abilities has God given you?" Are you using them to minister to God? For example, it is sad for those who have lovely singing voices never to use them in private alone with God. I have a decent singing voice, and I often use my voice to sing alone to my Best Friend. He gave me the voice, and I use it to minister to Him. I have a writing ability, and I use it to write in a journal messages directed to the One Who gave me my ability. I have a love for the use of words, especially when those words are used to encourage people. Daily, I use my words to voice my praise and my love to Jesus.

Jesus found a very sick lady when he entered Peter's house. Some folks who cared sought Jesus so that He could help her. With simply the touch of His hand, this woman's fever was gone. But the sweetest part of this story to me is this statement: *"and she arose, and ministered unto them."* (Matthew 8:15b)

Jesus has often found me in need of healing. With simply the touch of His hand, Christ has healed a lot of sickness and a lot of pain in my life. He has left me with ability where once there was nothing but weakness. What should I do with my healing? I should immediately use it to minister to those around me, especially to the One Who brought it to me in the first place. How foolish to squander our gifts and our teachings on worldly and selfish pleasures! May we all do what Peter's mother-in-law did. Let's give it all back to God!

Worthy to See the Miracles

A Lesson From the Daughter of Jairus

"*But when Jesus heard it, he answered him, saying, Fear not:
believe only, and she shall be made whole.
And when he came into the house, he suffered no man to go in,
save Peter, and James, and John,
and the father and the mother of the maiden.*"
(Luke 8:50, 51)

Chapter 5
The Daughter of Jairus
Matthew 9:18 -26; Mark 5:21 -43;
Luke 8:41 -56

A RULER OF THE synagogue had a 12-year-old daughter who was at the point of death. The ruler, Jairus, fell at Jesus' feet and besought Him to heal her. Unlike the centurion who said in Matthew 8:8, "...*Lord, I am not worthy that thou shouldest come under my roof: but speak the word only, and my servant shall be healed,*" Jairus desired the Lord to come to his house. He did not quite possess the faith which the centurion did. "*When Jesus heard it, he marvelled, and said to them that followed, Verily I say unto you, I have not found so great faith, no, not in Israel.*" (Matthew 8:10)

Jesus, along with Peter, James and John, headed to Jairus' house. On the way, some folks stopped them and said that the daughter was now dead. They assumed there was no longer reason for Jesus to continue His journey. Jesus encouraged Jairus by saying, "...*Be not afraid, only believe.*"

When Jesus came to the house, He found people weeping and wailing. He asked them why they made such a fuss, because the damsel was not dead but only sleeping. The people responded to Jesus' claim by laughing at Him and by scorning Him. So Jesus sent them all out of the room except for Jairus, his wife, and the three disciples.

Jesus took the damsel by the hand and said, "...*Maid, arise.*" She arose and began to walk. Jesus admonished the parents to tell no man and to give the damsel something to eat.

In this story, we find lessons, not only about praying for our children, but also about praying for those who are in need. We find lessons on what it takes to be one of the few folks who really sees prayers answered and witnesses miracles performed in their prayer lives.

(1) **Seek the Lord humbly.** Jairus traveled some distance to kneel before Jesus' feet and to ask Jesus to heal his daughter. He had enough sense to know where to go, and he cared enough to go there. Surely we can take the time to kneel before the ever-present God on behalf of His people.

Though I believe a person can pray anywhere and at any time, I have a scheduled time daily when I kneel before the Lord. I remind the Lord that I am kneeling before Him as evidence that I am humbling myself before Him and that I realize my weakness and His greatness. I worship and praise the Lord first, as well as seeking forgiveness for my sins. Then I seek Him on behalf of my family and others.

I call many people's names before the Lord each week in many different ways. I have a scheduled day when I pray for the following categories of people:

Sunday — those I know grieving the loss of a loved one

Monday — my husband's friends and my friends
(We have them all over the country.)

Tuesday — the sick
(There are a few sick folks for whom I pray daily and others for whom I pray at a scheduled time each week.)

Thursday — pastors

Friday — missionaries

Saturday — troubled or broken marriages of those whom I know and love

These are the areas for which I pray daily:

- my husband and our marriage
- my children
- my family
- my husband's family

- my country
- my church
- the unsaved

Though I am not the perfect example of what a prayer warrior should be, you can see that I seek the Lord very often on behalf of very many people.

2 **Seek the Lord diligently when others discourage you.** People said to Jairus, "...*Thy daughter is dead: why troublest thou the Master any further?*" (Mark 5:35) But Jairus continued to follow Jesus to the house where his daughter lay. I have been told on occasion that something I was praying about was too small and insignificant to take to the Lord. Still, I believe with all of my heart that God is interested in everything. I would rather be guilty of taking too much to the Lord (if that is possible) rather than too little. I want the answer to be in God's will, of course, and even more so as I get older. But I take everything to Him.

3 **Do not give up hope when others have.** Many years ago I was told by a close friend that a particular request for which I had been praying for years would never come true. I continued praying—for 22 years to be exact. It did come true in a greater way than I had ever imagined.

4 **Believe!** Believe when others are scorning in disbelief. People laughed at Jesus when He said the damsel was sleeping. Because of this, Jesus sent them out of the room; and they missed seeing one of the most magnificent answers to prayer of all time. Jairus and his wife, however, were allowed to stay. Why? I don't believe it was because Jairus had a lot of faith. But he had enough faith to believe when others did not. He had enough faith to prevent him from becoming cynical when things were going wrong. When those around him were becoming cynical, Jairus' faith sustained him.

It is no wonder that so many Christians are miserable. Their unbelief and their poor prayer life have hindered them from witnessing all of the miracles and answers to prayer that God has for them. I truly enjoy life! I think one of the main reasons is that I am walking with Christ each day. Each day I am observing in big and small ways how Jesus is answering prayer and working in each situation of my life. When you sow in prayer, you reap in witnessing evidence of God's work in your life and in the lives of those for whom you pray. When you see God at work, you find big and small miracles on display every day for your personal entertainment. How exciting life can be for the praying wife and mother!

5 **Ask God to revive the spirit of others.** My dad once preached a sermon on standing in the gap for others through our love and through our prayers. He mentioned how no person would die spiritually if he had someone who cared enough to stand in the gap for him. I stand in the gap for literally hundreds of people each week as I call their names in prayer. I stand in the gap for my parents, my husband and my children each day. Would all of these folks make it anyway, even if they did not have my praying for them? I do not wish to find out. I believe that my prayers help to keep them going in the right direction, and it is this faith (which is sometimes weak) that keeps me praying for them.

I also pray for God to revive my own spirit. Allow me to insert here a little three point outline which we find in the story of Jairus' daughter. This will help us to learn how to have our own spirits revived on a daily basis.

A. *Wait for God's touch.* Jesus took the damsel by the hand, and He revived her spirit. Daily I seek the Lord in Bible reading, Bible memorization and in prayer; and I wait for Him to touch me. As one famous preacher said, "I read the Bible each day until my heart burns." I do the same, and I never go away disappointed. We miss so many miracles and so much revival when we do not wait for God's touch through daily devotional time.

B. *Listen for God's voice.* Jesus said to the damsel, "...*Arise.*" The damsel heard Jesus' voice and, at the sound of His voice, her spirit was revived. I not only take my prayers to God, but I also listen for His answer. I believe that God answers **every** prayer that I pray. If I pray for a new Cadillac and I do not receive one, I do not become disillusioned in my prayer life. Perhaps my old car breaks down instead. God's answer to our prayer may sometimes be "no." We often miss revival in our lives because we only listen for the answer we are waiting to hear. Even though the answer may not be as we had wished, hearing God's voice and knowing He is at work is always exciting. Our spirit misses so much when we do not listen for God's voice.

I have been praying for a special need I see in a friend's life. God has answered my prayer by causing something to happen which will put distance between my friend and me. Though God's answer to prayer has left me personal pain in this situation, I can't help but be excited about what I believe God is doing in my friend's life.

C. *Obey God's command.* The damsel obeyed God's command to arise, and her spirit was revived. I, too, want to obey God's command though at times they may seem to be a drudgery. There are so many miracles available to those who obey God's commands.

I wish every wife could realize that God has more miracles waiting for her if she will obey His commands such as, "Wives, submit." The world would tell us that submission to a husband is drudgery. But obeying this command (and all of God's commands) is the key which unlocks the spirit and allows us to witness miracles.

(6) **Live worthy of God's presence and of His miracles every day.** I admire Jairus and his wife for being counted worthy of witnessing this one miracle which Jesus performed. But I admire even more Peter, James, and John who were the only other people present when Jairus' daughter was raised from the dead. Why? Because they stayed close to Jesus every day. Jairus and his wife had enough sense to seek Jesus when they needed Him. But Peter, James and John stayed very close to Him every day. In doing so, they probably witnessed most of the miracles which Jesus performed when He was on this earth. They also were able to witness the miracles that Jesus performed **through** them after Jesus' ascension into Heaven.

Though I am the daughter of one powerful preacher and the wife of another one, much of my life is spent alone with God. I want to be close to Him **every** day, even when no one sees. I do not have to get prayed up when trials come. Nor do I have to seek the Lord quickly when a special conference is coming and I will be speaking before many people. I have a special relationship with Christ which continues day by day; every day of my walk with Him is as exciting as the opening day of our Pastors' School at First Baptist Church of Hammond, Indiana. I've seen some miraculous things in crowded places. But by staying close to my Lord, I have seen some pretty miraculous things today even though it is just He and I in my house right now.

I need to feel and to see God at work in my life **every** day in order to continue to grow in my spirit. Yesterday's blessings, great as they were, are simply not enough. I need to see miracles in my life and in the lives of so many others for whom I pray. I want to believe and to live and to listen, so that God would count me worthy to see His miracles. I would not want my disbelief or my cynical attitude to hinder what God could do for me, for my family, and for those I love.

"Lord, Please make me worthy—make my readers worthy—of see-ing Your miracles not only in our lives, but perhaps even more so in the lives of those whose names we call before You each day. Lord, revive our spirits and theirs. Amen."

Convicting Power

A Lesson From Herodias

"Who knoweth the power of thine anger?
even according to thy fear, so is thy wrath."
(Psalm 90:11)

Chapter 6
Herodias
Matthew 14:1-14; Mark 6:14-29

KING HEROD LIVED in fear and guilt because he had beheaded a man whom he feared and respected. He had beheaded a man whom he believed to be holy and just. He had beheaded a man whose preaching he enjoyed hearing and following. Why had he beheaded such a man as John the Baptist? Because his wife had influenced him to do it.

King Herod kept hearing about a man Who was raising the dead, casting out devils and healing the sick. Though this man was Jesus, the Son of God, Herod believed Him to be John the Baptist risen from the dead, evidence that Herod did indeed live in fear.

Herodias is an excellent example of what happens when a woman uses her constraining power over a man in a wrong way. Allow me to share with you step by step exactly where this disaster began and where it ended.

1 **It began with greed.** Herodias divorced her husband to marry her brother-in-law. Why? I believe it was because he was the king. Her marriage was not based on love or commitment. It was not based on a desire to **be** a help, but rather on a desire to receive help for herself. The marriage began with the wife asking, "How can I use my power to get from my husband what I want?"

This is an attitude too prevalent in today's marriages, even Christian marriages. Many women say, "I'll get from my husband what I want and, if he doesn't give me what I want, I'll divorce him and find another." The more acceptable way of saying this is: "My husband just isn't meeting my needs." Allow me to share with you where this attitude leads.

(2) **Greed led to divorce and adultery.** Divorce and adultery, though more commonly accepted in Christian circles today, is still the result of greed or selfishness on the part of one or both of the partners. That selfishness often progresses as the dissatisfied partner neglects the children and begins to date around.

I have no desire to hurt those who are divorced. It is only by God's grace and mercy that I am still a happily married woman. I pray weekly for those I know who are divorced, many against their own will. But divorce is a disease which the Devil has spread into God's churches. It grieves me that divorce destroys homes, which destroys churches, which destroys nations. It also grieves me that divorce usually leads to more sin and heartache, not only in the lives of the divorced partners, but also in the lives of their children. I honestly do not feel judgmental toward divorced people, but I do feel very judgmental toward divorce: I hate it! Allow me to continue.

(3) **Divorce and adultery led to conviction.** In God's mercy, He sent a preacher to help King Herod. God sent a wonderful and a humble man called John the Baptist. Having read of John the Baptist, I do not believe he preached to Herod and Herodias in a noncompassionate way. He was a humble man, but he believed that right was right and wrong was wrong. He had the courage to tell the King himself.

The Bible tells us that King Herod respected John the Baptist. He knew he was holy. He enjoyed hearing John the Baptist, and he often gladly followed what he taught him. Perhaps, Herod even considered making the situation right with Herodias, but Herodias would not have such a thing.

4 **Conviction led to anger.** It is evident to me that Herodias also felt convicted by John the Baptist and by his preaching. But she did not respond to conviction properly as Herod did, through obedience. Rather, she responded to conviction with anger. This is often the response of the Christian woman to conviction: "Who does that preacher think he is? He's judging me!"

May I respond to these ladies by saying this: Right is right, and wrong is wrong and sometimes the most compassionate people are those who would tell you so. I am not saying that we should go around preaching sermons when it is not our place. Usually that is only the job of God-called preachers. But we should not allow the anger of others to water down our convictions.

Anger is never the proper response to conviction.

5 **Anger led to more gross sin.** Herodias' anger led to rebellion which eventually led to murder. Usually when a woman becomes angry at the man of God and tries to destroy him, it is because she feels conviction about some sin in her life. Often, then, she uses her family to help her to hurt the man of God.

Herodias devised a scheme. Her daughter had danced an enchanting dance before King Herod. Herodias heard that her daughter could have whatever she wanted after performing wickedly before the king. Herodias admonished her daughter that what she wanted was the death of John the Baptist.

Herodias would not be satisfied to just hear that John the Baptist was dead. She wanted to see his head and to have it placed as a trophy on a wooden board. How grotesque were her desires! When a woman responds improperly to conviction, she loses her femininity and becomes increasingly hardhearted.

6 **Gross sin leads to the destruction of others.** John the Baptist did indeed lose his life on earth, but he gained rewards in Heaven. Herod, however, lived in fear and guilt. Herodias' daughter was punished worst of all because she lived under the influence of a mother who was motivated by greed, selfishness, and anger.

We must all realize how much we hurt those we love when we seek to hurt those we feel we hate. One of the greatest lessons I have ever learned from my parents is to love my enemies. This lesson has freed me from bitterness and from the sins to which bitterness leads. One of the greatest things I can do for my children is to love those who would seem to be my enemies.

Another great lesson I can pass on to my children is to have great respect for the man of God. It is so easy to say "Amen" to the man of God when he is preaching against a sin which I have not committed. But I get tired of him "harping" about my sins. He is always "harping" about going soul winning and helping others. He doesn't know my situation. He probably doesn't understand how shy and really busy I am.

More often I am reminded that he is teaching me how to live. I am a happy person today. I do not need tranquilizers such as Valium to make me so. Why? Because for 36 years a man of God named Dr. Jack Hyles has been telling me right is right and wrong is wrong, even when it was very humbling for him to have to do so. I have been convicted, and praise the Lord, when I have been angered, I have instead responded by hearing him gladly and by doing the things which he has taught me.

Thank you, dear preachers, all of you, who like my husband and my father, clearly tell us right is right and wrong is wrong. May we see in you the humility and the compassion which you truly possess, and may we give to you the honor which a man like John the Baptist deserved.

"Lord, help us to teach our children—no, help us to show them— how to respond properly to conviction. Amen."

Praying for Your Children

A Lesson From the Syrophenician Woman

"And she answered and said unto him, Yes, Lord:
yet the dogs under the table eat of the children's crumbs.
And he said unto her, For this saying go thy way;
the devil is gone out of thy daughter."
(Mark 7:28, 29)

Chapter 7

The Syrophenician Woman
Matthew 15:21-28; Mark 7:24-30

*I*N MATTHEW 15:21-28 AND again in Mark 7:24-30, an account is given about a woman who came to Jesus, falling at His feet and asking for healing for her demon-possessed daughter. This is the only story in the Bible of a parent praying for her child's spiritual welfare, and many lessons can be learned in this story about how a mother should pray for her child. Allow me to share them with you.

(1) **In order to pray for her child properly, a mother should recognize her enemy.** Some readers may not believe that this story applies to them and to their child because the daughter in this story was demon-possessed. Now believe me, I am **not** trying to insinuate that your children or mine are demon-possessed—though I have seen some who acted like it, especially two year olds.

However, it is the Devil who is our child's enemy. Our enemy is not really the wrong crowd. The enemy is not even rock music or drugs. Our enemy is the Devil, the worldly system which he controls, and the flesh of our children which the Devil would **like** to control.

This is why each morning, usually in the early morning hours, I pray and ask God to bind the Devil and not to allow him to have any power or authority upon my children's lives. Probably my children will be tempted—even Jesus was tempted. But I believe the Syrophenician woman is an example to us, in teaching us that we ought to pray a hedge of protection from the Devil around our children.

Parents also need to remember that their children's leaders are not their enemy. Sometimes a well-meaning Christian school teacher or youth director may make a decision which seems to be hindering rather than helping a mother to rear her child. Still that mother should support rather than fight those leaders. She should realize that it is the Devil who tries to divide the different authorities in our children's lives. He is the one we should fight, and prayer is our most powerful weapon against him.

(2) **In order to pray for her child properly, a mother should pray humbly.** Jesus loved the Syrophenician woman even though He was a Jew and this woman was a Greek who was looked down upon by the Jews. When the disciples asked Jesus to send this woman away, Jesus responded to them by asking them to send for her.

But Jesus' response to this woman was very different. He called the Syrophenician woman a dog. Mark 7:27 tells us, *"But Jesus said unto her, Let the children first be filled: for it is not meet to take the children's bread, and to cast it unto the dogs."* Jesus was saying that His favored children (the Jews) should receive His miracle and blessing and not the Gentiles of which she was a part.

There is an old saying which reads, "Sticks and stones can break my bones, but words can never harm me." While I believe this saying to be true, I still would feel "harmed" if my Saviour called me a dog. (Come to think of it, being a Gentile, I guess He did!)

The Syrophenician woman responded humbly. Mark 7:28, *"And she answered and said unto him. Yes, Lord: yet the dogs under the table eat of the children's crumbs."* She responded by saying, "Yes, Lord. Yes, I am a dog." This mother was humble as she prayed for her daughter.

For many years, I prayed to the Lord for my children by saying things like this:

"Dear Lord, You know I have tried hard to be a good mother. You know how hard I work to do what You want me to do. Please help my children to turn out right."

This, I believe, is a wrong way to pray. I was proud in my prayers and trying to impress God with my parenting skills which, by the way, I could never do. Since studying the life of the Syrophenician woman, my prayers are more like this:

> "Dear Lord, be merciful to me a sinner. I know I could never be all a mother should be, but I trust Your mercy, and I ask You to protect my children from the Devil and help them to turn out right."

In other words, I used to pray more like the Pharisees, but I am learning to pray more like the sinner that I am.

Another thing which I think helps me to pray more humbly is having a scheduled time each week when I call out many, many names of the children of my friends and of my peers in the ministry to the Lord. My prayer for my children to turn out right is not a prayer to impress others with my mothering skills. Neither is it a prayer which I hope will guarantee that my children turn out better than anyone else's children. I am pulling for my children and I am pulling for the children of others.

(**3**) **In order to pray for her child properly, a mother should pray in faith.** The Syrophenician woman demonstrated her faith in three ways through her prayer.

First of all, when God hurt her feelings and did something which she may have found hard to understand, she said, **"Yes, Lord."** She agreed with God.

Many parents do not see their prayers answered for their children because they are in disagreement with God. God allows something to happen in their lives which hurts them. Perhaps they or someone they love becomes seriously ill. Perhaps another person hurts them, perhaps even a preacher. They become bitter against God, and in their bitterness, God does not answer their prayers. They lose their children because of an ugly thing like bitterness.

Parents often fail to realize that their best opportunity to transfer their faith in Jesus and to prove His superiority over what the Devil has to offer is when trials come. Some of the worst children I have ever met are preachers' kids. However, some of the best children I have ever met are the children of a pastor and his wife who have been through a church split. Why? I believe it is because they have had the opportunity to watch their parents go through trials and have seen them say without bitterness, "Yes, Lord."

I have had the opportunity to see my parents go through situations where God might have seemed to be unkind, and I have seen the response of my parents. They have said, "Yes, Lord; whatever God does is best, and God is always good." I am grateful for their example in this way. It has helped to transfer their faith to me and to make me more what I ought to be for God.

Secondly, the Syrophenician woman displayed her faith by believing that God had something for her. She said, "...Yet the dogs under the table eat of the children's crumbs." This mother humbly recognized her own weaknesses, yet she still believed that God wanted to answer her prayer and that God had a miracle for her.

It is sometimes difficult for me to have faith that my children could be used of God with a mother like me...but then I remember the Syrophenician woman and I tell God that I believe that He will answer my prayers. I believe that God wants us to take the time each day not only to ask for things, but also to express our faith in Him. He wants us to brag on Him and to express to Him our belief in what He can do for our children.

Thirdly, this mother displayed her faith by continuing to seek Jesus when others tried to turn her away. The disciples tried to stop her from seeing Jesus. But she pressed on for her daughter's sake! When others don't believe in you or in your children, keep praying. When others would discourage you from seeking Jesus' face about something, when they would try to convince you the situation is hopeless, keep on praying.

Jesus Himself seemed to hesitate to answer her prayer. But she pressed on! Her daughter was far away from her presence. But she pressed on! What an encouragement to the parents of wayward children, who may not even know where their child is.

When the woman finished her plea to Jesus, He answered her prayer. Mark 7:29, *"And he said unto her, for this saying go thy way; the devil is gone out of thy daughter."* Jesus answered her prayer because of what she said. Surely then we would want to learn what she said. Again, her statement was: *"...Yes, Lord: yet the dogs under the table eat of the children's crumbs."*

She responded with humility and she responded with faith. *"And when she was come to her house, she found the devil gone out, and her daughter laid upon the bed."* (Mark 7:30) Jesus answered this mother's prayer for her daughter. It is with humility and with faith that we also can see our prayers answered for our children.

> *"Lord, I believe that You can give our children protection from the Devil and that You can use them and make them all that You would have them to be. I ask You to do exactly that for my children and for the children of others. Amen."*

Giving It All

A Lesson From the Widow's Mite

"For all they did cast in of their abundance;
but she of her want did cast in all that she had,
even all her living."
(Mark 12:44)

Chapter 8
The Widow's Mite
Mark 12:41-44; Luke 21:1-4

*I*N THIS STORY Jesus sat and watched people cast their money into the treasury. He observed many rich people putting a lot of money into the offering. Then He saw a poor widow throw two mites into the treasury.

Jesus was so impressed by this woman's offering and the lesson therein that on the spur of the moment (or so it seems) He called His disciples to Himself. He pointed out to the disciples that this poor widow had cast in more than all of the others who had given, because she had given her all.

This story reminds me of a Mother's Day I once celebrated. This is the only Mother's Day when my husband was out of town, and I found myself dealing with some self-pity.

I got out of bed early as I always do on Sunday mornings, and I began to get ready for church. After I had been up for quite a while, my two children came to me and asked me to get back in bed. Because I was already dressed for church, I hesitated to obey their request. Suspecting they were up to something, I obeyed and headed toward the bedroom.

When I entered the bedroom, I saw a big sign across the headboard which said, "Happy Mother's Day!" After I got back in bed, my children proceeded to bring me their homemade breakfast. I had already taught my daughter how to prepare some breakfast items; yet, what she and her brother chose to feed me for breakfast was interesting, to say the least.

Giving It All

My breakfast consisted of saltine crackers, cheddar cheese, nacho-cheese flavored potato chips, chocolate chip cookies, and milk. I guess my children served me what, in their hearts, they had always desired for breakfast.

I did not fuss at them, however, for the lack of nutritional value in such a breakfast. Instead, I ate every bite of my breakfast, and to this day, I have never had a meal which tasted any better. Why? Though my children lacked the knowledge to make me a gourmet breakfast, they had given me something much more valuable. They had given me their hearts and their love. They had given me their all!

I couldn't help but think about this breakfast throughout the entire day. I thought of how good God is to give me the love of my children. More than that, though, I thought of how good God is to accept the gifts I bring to Him.

Ten months later I wrote my first book, *A Wife's Purpose*. The response I received to that book was surprising to me and sometimes overwhelming. But God had provided the perfect story for me to remember to keep my head from swelling with pride.

Each time someone commented about my book, I remembered my breakfast in bed. I reminded myself that the most profound thought I could ever think or put on paper is like junk food in God's sight. Yet He takes it and uses it, not because of my greatness, but because He wants to give us opportunity to give and to serve Him. He accepts our talents and what we have to give, but all He wants from us is a heart full of love.

On that Mother's Day of several years ago now, I wrote the following poem:

Meekly and humbly I give my life,
Like a child who has nothing more to bring.
Sweetly and kindly You accept my gift,
Like a mother who wants no better thing.

My life is one, small thing.
It's all I have to bring.
But You'll take my small thing,
For all You wanted is my heart.

As I read the story of the widow's mite, I was again reminded of that delicious meal of junk food which was served by two very special people. I was reminded of what I received from my children and of what God wants to receive from us. And I learned some very valuable lessons.

(1) Those who are lacking are better able to give their all to God. We should not be discouraged if we find that we are lacking in certain areas of our lives. Nor should we be impatient if we find that our husbands or our children are lacking when compared with others. God is better able to use those who are lacking.

"For ye see your calling, brethren, how that not many wise men after the flesh, not many mighty, not many noble, are called:

But God hath chosen the foolish things of the world to confound the wise; and God hath chosen the weak things of the world to confound the things which are mighty;

And base things of the world, and things which are despised, hath God chosen, yea, and things which are not, to bring to nought things that are:

That no flesh should glory in his presence."

(I Corinthians 1:26-29)

God could not use the rich people to be a Biblical example of giving. Not everyone could be helped by them. He needed someone who lacked.

I could not have felt as loved if my children had been gourmet cooks. I needed their lack of knowledge to show me what was in their hearts.

2 **God wants our weaknesses more than He wants our talents.** God wants what we are lacking—not what we have in abundance. God was pleased with the widow for giving what she lacked more than with the rich people for giving what they had in abundance.

I have been told by many that I have a gift for writing, and I do believe this is an area of strength in my life. What God wants most from me is not my writing. He doesn't desire most what I have in abundance. God wants from me what I am lacking.

I lack in the area of faith. I do not trust people easily, perhaps because I have experienced people's hurting my parents in the ministry. It is hard for me to let go and to put my faith and my trust in God, especially in certain situations. But more than God wants me to use my writing for Him, He wants me to give Him my faith. The fact that I don't have faith in abundance only causes God to desire it more. When we give to God from what we lack, we give more than others who give from their abundance.

Readers, don't let what you are lacking stop you from serving God. Give to Him—especially where you lack. Mothers, teach your children that their lack does not need to hinder them spiritually. Wives, encourage your husband, especially in the area where He is lacking.

I wish that all wives and mothers would be more Christ-like and accept the lacks of their husbands and children as readily as they accept their strengths. I do not mean that mothers should allow their children to do wrong. But every mother should do a heap more praising and accepting than she does nagging and scolding.

Oftentimes, mothers are able to accept the lacks that they find in their small children. After all, weaknesses are cute at this age. Yet when their children become teenagers, mothers begin to pick at what their children are lacking. Why? Weaknesses in teenagers are often a source of embarrassment to mothers.

A mother should not worry about her image as a parent. She should do her best to train her children, especially when they are young. Then she should accept her children, knowing they will not be perfect just as their mother is not.

Though weaknesses are not very cute in a middle-aged husband, a wife should always accept her husband as he is. She should put the most emphasis upon accepting his weaknesses.

Let me also say that wives should give to their husbands what they are lacking. For example, if a wife is lacking in the area of being affectionate, she should not use this as an excuse for being cold. Rather, she should put special emphasis upon giving her husband her weakness and on being an affectionate wife.

My husband most appreciates my trust because he knows that this is an area where I am lacking. Though he is completely trustworthy, it is hard for me to give my trust to others.

(3) When we give our weakness to God, He notices. He also causes others to notice. Jesus noticed the widow's giving, and He pointed it out to His disciples. He wanted others to notice it also. Surely it grieves Jesus when He finds wives and mothers failing to notice the efforts of their loved ones in the areas where they are weak.

For example, if your child is lacking in the area of self-discipline, you should notice when he makes an effort to work hard and to be disciplined. If your husband is lacking in the area of tenderness, you should never take for granted his tender deeds, though they will probably be lacking to someone who is more tender. It is much easier to notice failure in others, especially in the areas where they are lacking. Praise in these areas, however, will encourage your loved ones to give more in the area where they are lacking.

(4) When we give of our lack to God, it causes us to depend upon Him. This widow was going to have to depend upon God more because she gave all she had. After she gave, she had nothing left. The rich people, though they had given much, had much left with which to take care of themselves.

I depend upon God in my writing because I believe it is the necessary and the right thing to do. I can, however, write a book without seeking the Lord much easier than I can put my trust in people without seeking His help. I have to beg God to help me to trust people. So which do you think God enjoys receiving more from me—my talent or my weakness? He desires my weakness because it causes me to depend on Him.

The worst thing that your husband or children could do is to try to make it on their own without God. Praise the Lord that your loved ones are not perfect. This will cause them to depend upon God, and it will also cause them to need you more. I often remind myself that if my family was perfect, they certainly wouldn't need me.

(5) Jesus does not want from others what they do not have. Jesus did not want millions from the poor widow. He was satisfied with her two mites because it was what she had. Wives and mothers are foolish to set expectations for their loved ones which are too high.

I have a vision for my husband and for my children which is limitless because our God is limitless. Humanly speaking, though, there is only so much my loved ones can accomplish in their lives. God may choose to use them in what would seem to me to be a small way. Though my vision for my loved ones and my faith in them is grand, it takes only something very small to please me. I just want them to do their best to please the Lord in their lives.

(6) God does not consider us to be careless when we give what we are lacking. I can imagine what we, as wives, would say if our husband gave our last two mites in the offering plate. "How in the world are we going to buy groceries this week? You are so reckless in your giving!" Of course, there is a practical side as well as a spiritual side to every situation. But wives should hesitate to criticize their loved ones for giving what they lack.

Guard against the following thoughts, and please don't form them into verbal statements:

- "My son is too lazy. He could never pastor a church."

- "My daughter is too shy. She couldn't be an effective soul winner."

- "My husband is a poor organizer. That's not the job for him."

Encourage your family when they give what they are lacking. My daughter, Jaclynn, is on fire for the Lord in the area of soul winning. However, she has struggled with her health. Her immune system and her energy level have been low. I often have to bite my tongue when I see her busy on the weekends with soul winning and with the bus route. I know there are times when the right thing to do is to stop her for a while. But I hesitate to stop her as she gives her energy to the Lord at a time when she is lacking in this area.

During the days of my youth, I remember my own parents expressing concern over my recklessness in the area of soul winning. I also remember how they encouraged me instead of discouraging me, though at times they worried about my safety and so forth.

7) **When we give our all to God, He notices and causes others to notice for generations to come.** Thousands of years later, the sound of two mites being dropped into the offering plate can still be heard. Why? Because a widow gave her all.

My dad, Pastor Jack Hyles, says, "God squeezes out of everyone everything He can." Wives and mothers, we should not cast aside our visions for our loved ones because we have been disappointed. Rather, we should squeeze out of them all the potential that we can. We do this by acceptance and praise and not by nagging.

We should squeeze out of our own lives everything that we can for the glory of God. Let's forget what we are lacking as Christians, as wives, and as mothers. Instead, let us give to God and to our loved ones all that we can. Let us give them what we are lacking. Let us give them our all!

Where Jesus Reveals Himself

A Lesson From Anna

"And she coming in that instant
gave thanks likewise unto the Lord,
and spake of him to all them
that looked for redemption in Jerusalem."
(Luke 2:38)

Chapter 9
Anna
Luke 2:36 - 38

ANNA WAS A very old and widowed prophetess of 84 years of age. She stayed in the temple day and night praying and fasting.

Eight days after Jesus' circumcision, Mary and Joseph brought Him to the temple at Jerusalem to present Him to the Lord. The Bible tells us that there was a Spirit-filled man named Simeon who lived in Jerusalem. The Holy Spirit had revealed to Simeon that he would not die until he had seen the Lord's Christ. The Holy Spirit led Simeon to be in the temple at the time that Jesus and His parents arrived. Simeon held the child Jesus in his arms and blessed God. Simeon then began to pray. He told the Lord that he was now ready to die because he had seen the salvation of God.

Simeon blessed this family and prophesied to them. He told Mary and Joseph that Jesus was *"…set for the fall and rising again of many in Israel; and for a sign which shall be spoken against;…that the thoughts of many hearts may be revealed."* (Luke 2:34, 35) Simeon also prophesied to Jesus' mother and to Joseph that they themselves would suffer much anguish because of what Jesus would have to go through.

As this prophesying and blessing was taking place, Anna entered into the scene. When Anna saw Jesus, she began to thank the Lord, and the Bible says that she told others who looked for redemption in Jerusalem about Jesus.

There are very few people to whom Jesus revealed Himself, especially during the first 33 years of His life. Yet Anna was one of those especially chosen ones.

I, too, need to have Jesus reveal Himself to me. I need His wisdom as I make decisions each day, and I need the leadership of His Holy Spirit in all I do. Because of this, I have analyzed the characteristics of Anna's life which allowed her to be chosen.

(1) **Anna was gracious.** The name *Anna* means "gracious." The word *gracious* means "showing kindness, polite, full of compassion and mercy, refined." I pray daily that the Holy Spirit will give me His compassion. It is so easy for Christians like myself to be smitten with the disease of complacency. Even worse is the disease that Job's friends had in the Bible. That is the disease of a judgmental or a critical spirit which causes us to analyze the reasons behind people's burdens rather than having compassion on them.

God will not reveal Himself to this type of person. He reveals Himself through the filling of His Spirit, and there is no room for the Spirit in the critical and judgmental heart. The Holy Spirit finds room in the compassionate heart.

(2) **Anna studied and taught the Bible.** So many are the Christians who seek revelation from the Lord apart from the written Word of God. God left us His Bible so that we might have instructions to follow in our Christian life on this earth. Many are the Christians today who obviously have strayed from the roles and standards clearly given in the Bible; yet, they are seeking and claiming some new revelation.

I believe that the Holy Spirit can reveal Himself to Christians today as tangibly as He did in Bible days. But I do not believe that He reveals things which are contrary to His written Word. I would hesitate to trust a revelation claimed by some person who does not appear in his lifestyle to be following God's Written Revelation.

As a Christian who desires the leading of the Holy Spirit in my marriage, child rearing, etc., I realize that the secret is to read and to know what the Bible already has to say and to apply each part to my own life as aptly as possible. When the Lord sees me doing this, He will give me added wisdom in decisions which are not specifically covered in the Bible.

Anna, however, did not hoard the knowledge which she discovered in the Bible. Instead, she shared her findings with others. I do not believe she was a deeper-life Christian who just went deeper and deeper into the Word. In fact, the Bible tells us to the contrary.

(3) Anna was a soul winner. The Bible tells us that she told about Jesus to all who looked for redemption. Just about every Jew was looking for redemption at this time, whether or not they would accept Jesus. Anna was a balanced Christian. She took time to really know the Bible, and she took time to be a soul winner. There seems to be a dearth of this type of Christian. When we do find wives and mothers who really love the Bible, they usually are critical of those less-knowledgeable zealots who aggressively witness for the Lord. On the opposite side of the coin, there are many Christian wives who are busy, busy, busy for the Lord, but have not developed the relationship with God's Word which He intended for them to have.

Jesus could reveal Himself to Anna because she had already been seeking Him for a long time. Actually seeing Him was just the next step of revelation. Jesus knew that He could trust Anna once she had seen Him to share Him with others. Jesus reveals Himself to those who are already revealing what they know about Him to others.

This is worded much more aptly and concisely in Proverbs 11:30b where the Bible says, *"and he that winneth souls is wise."* I need Jesus to reveal Himself and His wisdom to me in my life, my marriage and in my child rearing. Therefore, I must be a soul winner, and I must find a way to share with others what He has revealed to me in His Word thus far.

(4) Anna was faithful to prayer and fasting. What a balanced lady! The compassionate side of Anna shows us that she must have been a "people" person, at least enough so to be kind toward others. Yet she had a wonderful relationship not only to the Bible and to soul winning, but her prayer life was acceptable also. Most

Christians want God's leadership upon their lives and in their families, but few are the Christian women who are willing to pay the necessary price. We pray quick prayers between television programs and then trust our feelings to guide us. Consequently, we fail in our Christian lives and then blame God for having led us to do things which are directly contrary to the Bible.

Ladies who make the right choices and who seem to have the mind of Christ are not so by accident. They have spent literally hours upon their knees in prayer and have been sacrificing meals and other things in order to know God's will.

5 **Anna praised the Lord.** Each morning before I ask for God's wisdom, I praise Him for a little while. It is only natural that we, as humans, give more attention and gifts to those who express their appreciation the most. Because I am made in the image of God, I get His attention by saying thank you to Him. I thank Him every day, as Anna did, for revealing Himself to me and for leading me the day before.

6 **Anna built her life around the church.** When people stop attending church, they usually claim that they are closer to God than ever before. "After all," they claim, "God is everywhere!"

But it is not coincidental that they lower their standards, and their lives usually, if not always, begin to fall apart when they leave church? Why? Because the assembly of God's people is a Biblical revelation. My husband has taught me that God most often uses a man to reveal His truth. Men like Abraham, Moses, Joshua, Elijah, etc. were used in the Bible in a special way to reveal God's truths to God's people.

God must have known that His people would need a leader, someone with skin on him, someone we could see and hear. God uses that leader and the assembly of God's people to reveal much of His truth. When we are not faithful to church, the influences of the world and of our own flesh overpower the influence of God's man and God's people, and we begin to make wrong decisions. Our lives, our marriages, our families begin to fall apart.

When we listen to God's Word through God's man on a regular basis and when we seek the influence and fellowship of God's people, God uses them to reveal Himself to us. He also reveals Himself through His Spirit as He sees the sincere seeking of truth through this type of obedience. How good God is to use Christians to reveal Him to each other. I want to be in church not only so that I might see Christ revealed, but also so that I might reveal Him to others.

(7) **Anna was aged.** I have always had a special affection for older people. I must confess that I am tempted toward aversion to younger folks who do not display compassion for the aged. God definitely reveals Himself in a special way to those who are older. The wife and mother who wants to see Jesus revealed ought to seek wisdom from older women whom she admires. This type of learning is promoted in Titus 2:3, 4 where the Bible tells us, *"The aged women likewise, that they be in behaviour as becometh holiness, not false accusers, not given to much wine, teachers of good things; That they may teach the young women to be sober, to love their husbands, to love their children, To be discreet, chaste, keepers at home, good, obedient to their own husbands, that the word of God be not blasphemed."*

I want as a young woman to develop the type of character which would cause me to be qualified to teach others when I am aged. Aged women, take heed! Don't use aging as an excuse for becoming old and crabby. Use your older years instead to seek the Lord in a special way and to reveal Him to others as only you who have the experience can do.

(8) **Anna was lonely.** Anna was a widow. How special God is in that He reveals Himself so often to those who are lonely. He reveals Himself to all of us the most when we are the loneliest. Are you a widow? Are you a forsaken or divorced wife? Are you childless? Are you the wife of a busy preacher? Are your children grown?

WHERE JESUS REVEALS HIMSELF

Are you lonely? Don't use this as an excuse for becoming bitter. Instead do what Anna did. Use those quiet times to seek to know Jesus and His will. Then reveal Him to others.

There really is not all that much said about Anna; yet in a few short verses, we learn a lot about where Jesus reveals Himself.

"Dear Lord, I need to see You and to know Your will in my marriage, in my child rearing and in every aspect of my life. Help me to be in the right place at the right time so that You might choose to reveal Yourself to me. May I reveal You to others. Amen."

What Single Women Have That I Don't Have

A Lesson From a Widow

"*For thy Maker is thine husband;
the* LORD *of hosts is his name;
and thy Redeemer the Holy One of Israel;
The God of the whole earth shall he be called.*"
(Isaiah 54:5)

Chapter 10
A Widow
Luke 7:11 - 18

$\mathcal{I}$N LUKE CHAPTER seven, Jesus saw a man who had just died being carried out. Jesus saw His mother, who was a widow, weeping; and He saw many people surrounding her. When the Lord saw her, He had compassion on her and told her to "...*Weep not.*"

Jesus went to the young man and told him to arise. The dead man sat up and began to speak. Jesus delivered him to his mother. In this story, God gave something and did something very special for a lady, I believe, just because she was single. There is still something which God gives a single lady which I do not have.

$\left(\underline{1}\right)$ **A single lady has a special compassion from God that I don't have.** Many multitudes thronged Jesus while He was on this earth. Yet He only performed miracles for a just a few. Why did He perform a miracle for this widow? There is no record that she even sought for Jesus' help. I believe that Jesus chose to work a miracle for her just because He knew that she was alone. Jesus' life on this earth was alone and lonely. "*And it came to pass, as he was alone praying, his disciples were with him....*" (Luke 9:18a) The Bible tells us that Jesus often felt alone, even in crowds. I am not single, but I understand this feeling. As the daughter of the pastor of the world's largest church, I am very familiar with what it is like to be in huge crowds...and to feel like you are still alone. I am a loner, and it is not easy for me to feel that I fit in with a crowd.

The single woman feels this way often. She is often in crowds which consist mostly of families—a mother, a father and children. She may be a part of that crowd, but she does not fit in. She feels alone. Jesus has a special compassion for this type of a woman. I, as a married lady, do not have exactly what she has.

 A single woman has a special security from God that I don't have. She has a special knowledge of from where that security comes.

I believe in marriage! I believe it is a perfect God-ordained institution. I believe that every Christian woman should be preparing and should be willing to be a wife. Because I believe this, I may give some the idea that I look down on the single life. This is far from the truth.

I know there are some whom God wills to be single. And I know there is a special wisdom they possess which I do not.

I find a tremendous amount of security in the people with whom I share the four walls of my home. *"God setteth the solitary in families."* (Psalm 68:6a) I am one of those loners who has found great security in my family, and, in particular, my husband. If there is a husband in the world who can provide enough security for a wife, it is Jack Schaap. But he cannot…no human being can provide complete security for another. The single lady knows that better than anyone.

When I hear of a broken marriage or of some other human tragedy, I am tempted to find my security in my husband. I am tempted to whine and to try to lean upon him too heavily. I am tempted to find support from him which I should be seeking from the Lord. The single lady does not have this temptation.

I am not saying that a married lady should not make her husband feel that he is her security. But when a married lady seeks too much of her security in her husband and not in her relationship with Christ, she becomes even more insecure than she would have been had she stayed single.

 A single lady has a special joy that I don't have. She has the knowledge to know from where that joy comes. Christ Himself tells the single lady to "...*Weep not.*" Again, I find much joy in my marriage. True joy, though, comes from dependence upon God. There is a joy that I miss because there are areas where I don't feel the need to depend upon God as others do. I have my husband and my family to depend on. I'm not saying that I need God any less than anyone else, but I do not always feel that need as fully as the single lady does.

4 **A single lady has a special caretaker that I don't have.** God has given me a wonderful caretaker in my husband, Jack Schaap. But God does not leave the single lady without a caretaker. In every relationship of life where there is a void, God sends someone to fill that void.

A dear friend of mine backslid and went into sin, leaving a huge void in my life. It broke my heart. Yet, it has been sweet to see how God has sent some people to fill that void. Had I not lost fellowship with my friend, I could have not enjoyed in the same way those whom God sent to fill my void.

A married lady often does not enjoy other relationships as much as the single lady does. She is too busy enjoying and pleasing her husband and children. She often misses the depth of friendships which the single lady has.

God never leaves the single lady without a caretaker, someone who can fill the voids and meets the needs that a husband would fill. Sometimes that caretaker is a special person or group of people. Sometimes that caretaker is a special ministry which occupies her time and meets her needs. In some cases, however, there are voids which God does not choose to fill with a special person or with a special purpose. He chooses to fill them with Himself.

God cared for the widow in this story by restoring her son. He provided her son to be her caretaker and to fill the void in her life. Sometimes, God's provision for the single lady does not come by merely a human instrument. Instead, she experiences a special relationship with God.

A married lady can also have a sweet relationship with God. When the married lady is with her husband, she should seek him as if he were all she had. But when she is alone with God, she should seek Him as though she were a destitute widow. For you see, there is something special and unique about the relationship God has with the single lady.

5) **A single lady gives a special glory which I cannot give.** At this writing one of my best friends, Carol Frye, has never married. She probably is surprised that I would refer to her as a best friend. I spend very little time with her, so caught up am I in the care of my husband and children.

God chose to take the caretakers of Carol's life. He took her only sibling, her brother Keith, with multiple sclerosis. Several years later, God took her parents within six weeks of each other. He took her mother with brain cancer and her father with stomach cancer. God did not choose to restore these people to life.

Carol's suffering is, to me, very unique. Yet, she has responded with toughness. She has responded with joy and with unselfishness. I have discovered through this that Carol has a deep and abiding walk with Christ. I did not know before of that walk with Christ though I am sure it has existed. It is Carol's losses which have drawn my attention to the presence of Christ in her life.

Carol, of course, cries a lot. I think she is more soft and tender than she was before her losses. Yet she is a very joyful person. I notice her joy more than I notice the joy of others. Some people are joyful because life itself gives them reason to be. Some people have joy which is obviously a supernatural work of God. Their joy brings great glory to God. Such is the way with Carol's joy.

When I talk with Carol, I notice a relationship with Christ that I do not have. Yes, I am close to God. He is my friend, and I believe He would say that I am His friend—though not a very good one at times. I do not envy Carol's life, nor do I pity her. I realize that I have something she does not and that she has something that I do not.

To those who are single, like Carol, please do not feel that those who are married pity you or look down upon you. We may consider our husbands to be our greatest gift. But we are aware that you have something which we do not, which we cannot.

To those who are married, like myself, please do not ignore or look down upon the single lady. Please do not miss the lessons she has to teach. Rejoice each day in the husband and the family God has given you. Single ladies often wonder why you do not. But when you come before the Lord, seek Him as though you were the most destitute widow. Perhaps God has a little of that special compassion reserved for the single lady which He could bestow upon all of us.

"For thy Maker is thine husband; the LORD *of hosts is his name; and thy Redeemer the Holy One of Israel; The God of the whole earth shall he be called."* (Isaiah 54:5)

He Changed My Life

A Lesson From Mary Magdalene

"Wherefore I say unto thee, Her sins,
which are many, are forgiven; for she loved much:
but to whom little is forgiven, the same loveth little."
(Luke 7:47)

Chapter 11
Mary Magdalene
Luke 7:36-50; John 19:25; 20:1-18

ARY MAGDALENE WAS a woman possessed of seven devils—an immoral sinner who absolutely had her life transformed. Because Mary Magdalene had such a life-changing experience, she loved Jesus in an extraspecial way. In the book of Luke, there is an account of Mary Magdalene's anointing Jesus' feet with a very expensive ointment and wiping Jesus' feet with her hair and with her tears.

A Pharisee rebuked Jesus for allowing this sinful woman to touch Him. But Jesus revealed to him that Mary loved Jesus more because the Saviour had forgiven her more. Jesus did not consider her expensive gift of love to be a waste.

Mary showed her love and faithfulness to Jesus until the end of His earthly life. She followed Jesus and ministered to Him when He was in Galilee. She was present at Jesus' crucifixion and at His burial. She prepared Jesus' body for His burial with precious spices.

Mary Magdalene was one of the first people to whom Jesus appeared after He arose from the dead. I guess, like us, Jesus wanted to greet those first who He knew loved Him the most. Mary reacted to Jesus' appearance with fear and with great joy. It was her privilege to tell the disciples that Jesus had risen.

I would love to hear Mary Magdalene give her testimony! What a wonderful story to hear. She was truly a woman whose life began as one in deepest sin and ended in true love and usefulness for Christ. Jesus truly changed her life, and Mary Magdalene made a 180° turn. No wonder Mary Magdalene loved Jesus so much!

Oftentimes, preachers' kids and those who have grown up in a Christian home hesitate to give their testimonies. Why? Because they do not have one! They have no dramatic story to tell of immorality and demon-possession. They cannot become excited about a life that was transformed from darkness to light.

This, I believe, is a tragedy; and it is the reason why many preachers' kids do not grow to truly love the Lord with all of their hearts. They become unfaithful to Christ. Am I saying that all preachers' kids should experience deep sin so that they can love Jesus more? No, I **am** saying, however, that all preachers' kids should have testimonies to excite them. Every preacher's kid should have had his life changed 180° as Mary Magdalene did. Allow me to illustrate.

I was saved at the age of five years old. My mother won me to the Lord in the living room of our home. My salvation experience, only humanly speaking, of course, is unspectacular. I was not saved out of a life of deep sin, and I have not, to this day, experienced any sin which man would call "deep" sin. However, I still needed God to change my life—not just a little bit—but I needed to make a 180° change.

I began a quiet, unspectacular walk with the Lord when I was about eight years old. I stayed pretty faithful to that walk and that, I believe, is what kept me from deep sin. My life, though, still needed to be changed.

It was my sixth grade year in school when I remember beginning to feel a spiritual struggle taking place within me. During my junior high years, the struggle became deeper. During my freshman and sophomore years of high school, the fact that there was a spiritual rebellion taking place in my heart became evident to all who knew me.

I still read my Bible and prayed sporadically, and I stayed relatively close to my parents. For these things I praise the Lord. But my poor grades, my high number of demerits, my sometimes withdrawn and disruptive behavior displayed to those around me that God had not yet changed my life. My rebellion was evidenced in the friends I chose and in the boys I dated.

A Meek and Quiet Spirit

At the beginning of my junior year of high school, one of my earliest and closest friends was in a serious car accident. My friend, Sharon, was born six weeks before I was. Our mothers knew each other during their pregnancies. We were brought up in church together from infancy. We had remained friends all through school. We had even driven in a car pool together for most of our years we had attended our Christian school.

I had stopped riding in the car pool. I usually rode home with my sister who is two years older than me, or my mother drove me home. On the day of Sharon's accident, I remember my mother questioning whether she would be able to come to the school for me. She said if she wasn't able to pick me up, I should catch a ride in Sharon's car pool. As it turned out, my mother picked me up from school; and I was spared from being involved in the accident.

There were about ten people in the car, and all of them were taken to the hospital. The driver, a young man about 18, was killed. His fiancée was placed in critical condition, and my friend Sharon was also in critical condition. Sharon was in a coma and was pronounced dead four times that first day she was in the hospital.

The accident took place on the day before Thanksgiving which, of course, was a Wednesday. After the Wednesday evening service, my dad took me to the hospital to see Sharon for the first time. I believe that if my dad and my mom had not been there for me during this time, God would not have had the opportunity to work in my heart the way He did that night. I believe I would not have allowed God to do the work He did.

When I arrived home from the hospital, I went up to my bedroom window on the second story of our house. I looked out and saw that it was snowing outside. It was the first snow of the season which had caused the car accident. Even in Indiana, where snow is a pretty constant sight during the winter months, there is something mighty awesome about each year's first snow. The snow, indeed, looked awesome; the road in front of our house looked treacherous.

I looked at the snow, and I began to pray. I said something like this:

HE CHANGED MY LIFE

"Dear Lord,

I almost saw You tonight. If I had been in that car, I might have seen You. If I had seen You, I wouldn't have much to say to You. In my life so far, I have been given very much; and I have given very little in return.

It is hard for me, Dear Lord, to be a preacher's kid. I don't find it easy to do right and to be the example that I should be. So tonight, Lord, I stop trying. I give You my life, and I ask You to live Your life through me. You come and be the preacher's kid that I need to be.

Amen."

It was a simple and sincere prayer, and there was very little faith behind it. But on that November night, God changed my life—not a little bit—He turned me around 180°. I broke up with a boyfriend, not because he was a bad boy, but because we were not good for each other. I changed my friends. God provided strong Christian friends in a family with four daughters named the Foster family. God used them in a great way in my life at this time.

A year later, I wasn't dating anyone, and I was enjoying life for the first time in a while. My grades had gone up, and I had no demerits. (The year before I had over 100 demerits.)

One of the Hammond Baptist football players came to me one day and asked me this question: "Cindy, what happened to you?"

He said, "You've changed. You're not at all the person you used to be."

I walked away unembarrassed and very excited. God had truly worked a miracle in my life. He had changed me! Since that time, I have had a tremendous love for God. I cry easily, and my heart is tender, especially when I have the privilege of giving my testimony. You see, my testimony excites me every time I talk about it.

I have wonderful parents. They always did the best they could in rearing me, and they did an excellent job. If any person ever had a reason **not** to need her life changed, it was me. But there was a work that only God could do. I needed Him to do it. Since that life-changing experience in my life, the words of the following song have new meaning for me.

> I would love to tell you what I think of Jesus
> Since I found in Him a friend so strong and true;
> **I would tell you how He changed my life completely,**
> He did something that **no other friend could do.**
> No one ever cared for me like Jesus,
> There's no other friend so kind as He;
> **No one else could take the sin and darkness from me,**
> O how much He cared for me.
>
> – Charles Weigle

Now, I am rearing my own preacher's kids. My daughter and my son were both saved at four. To be honest, I wish they had not reached the time of accountability so early. But they were both obviously ready to be saved before their fifth birthdays. Their salvation experiences are unspectacular, humanly speaking. I won Jaclynn to the Lord in her bedroom. My husband won Kenny to the Lord in the car on Christmas day. Neither of my children were saved out of deep sin. They both make good grades, and they don't even have any demerits at this point. But God is going to have to change their lives. There is a work that they must allow Him to do, and I cannot do it for God or for them. That is why I prayed and asked God this morning, as I do so often, to do a work in their lives. I asked Him to do what I cannot do and to be what I cannot be.

I do try to work in my children's lives myself, but sometimes, I am smitten with what I call the "Barney Fife Syndrome." I mean that I take myself and my job a little too seriously. I say this to remind my readers that they must trust in God and not in themselves to rear their children. I say this to each preacher's kid so that he can better allow God to work in his life. Preachers' kids need to develop their own daily walk with Christ.

I especially say this to parents who have done their best and whose children have become unfaithful to Christ. It is not your fault. Sure, you have made some mistakes, and I would guess you have made some pretty serious ones. It is my experience as a parent that causes me to believe this. But if God were dependent upon our parenting skills alone, there would be no children who turned out to serve the Lord. The honest truth is that every child, and every adult for that matter, needs God to change his life.

Even this past Thursday, I drove around in the country alone with God for an hour and a half and begged Him to change my life in a certain area. I still need Him to do a work in me.

Jesus transformed Mary Magdalene, and He transformed me, and it wrought the following changes in our lives.

1 **It changed our values.** Mary Magdalene no longer valued expensive perfume or things that money could buy, as the Pharisees did. Her love for her Saviour was too great. Perhaps the preachers' kids who are living for this world and for material things need to have their lives changed.

2 **It changed our motives.** Mary Magdalene did what she could for Jesus, and He said that she had wrought a good work for Him. When Jesus changed my life, I became less the person who had to find attention through my humorous antics and more the person who wanted to quietly please my Lord.

3 **It changed our hearts.** Mary Magdalene displayed the tender heart of a child who had never known deep sin rather than the heart of a sin-hardened adulterer. She cried and washed the Saviour's feet with her tears. I cry more easily since God changed my life, and though I have not become near the Christian I should be, my heart is tender with love for Jesus.

4 **It changed our unfaithfulness.** Mary Magdalene stayed true to Jesus when those with cleaner pasts fled. She was faithful all the way through Jesus' death and resurrection. So many preachers' kids grow to be unfaithful to church, unfaithful to their parents and unfaithful to Christ. My prayer is that God will change their lives.

If you are a preacher's kid or anyone else for that matter and find that your life has not been changed, if you have no testimony to share of when your new life in Christ began; allow me to give you some advice found in Mary Magdalene's spectacular testimony.

A. *If you are not saved, put your faith in Jesus.* Be sure of your salvation experience. Being a preacher's kid doesn't make you a Christian.

B. *Repent of your sin.* Cry and become sorrowful for your own sin. I don't think Mary wept at Jesus' feet because she was thinking of how her parents had failed her. She wept because she had been delivered from her own sin.

C. *Humble yourself before God as Mary Magdalene humbled herself at Jesus' feet.* Quit being too proud to admit that your problem is that your life needs to be changed.

D. *Be honest with God.* Tell Him your negative feelings and inadequacies. He knows anyway. He'll come and live His life through you—I know this from experience.

E. *Quit valuing material things.* The only valuable "ointments" in life are those which are used for Jesus.

F. *Be faithful to what God has taught you thus far.* Be faithful to your church and to your parents.

G. *Do what you can.* Perhaps you cannot build the great work that your parents have built. I may be Jack Hyles' daughter, but I am no Jack Hyles. I don't compare myself with my parents. I love them for who they are, and I do what I can do for the Lord. Mary Magdalene did what she could and is remembered wherever the Gospel is preached. Do what you can, and you'll be remembered, too.

H. *Make Jesus your Master.* Mary Magdalene called Jesus her Master. We cannot make Jesus our Master through our own efforts. But we can allow Him to work in our lives, even when it hurts.

I guarantee you, preacher's kid, and I guarantee each and every reader, that if you will develop a daily walk with the Lord and if you will allow the Lord to change your life—He will! But I have to warn you—if God changes your life, your heart will be bursting with love for Him, and you'll have a hard time not wanting to give your spectacular testimony everywhere you go.

God changed my life—and I want Him to keep on changing me and changing me and changing me. He has much work yet to do. But He is working—and for that I love Him too deeply for words to possibly express.

Blessed Redeemer

A Lesson From
the Woman Loosed From Her Infirmity

"Bless the LORD, O my soul: and all that is within me,
bless his holy name. Who redeemeth thy life from destruction;
who crowneth thee with lovingkindness and tender mercies."
(Psalm 103:1, 4)

Chapter 12
The Woman Loosed from Her Infirmity
Luke 13:10 - 17

O N THE SABBATH DAY, Jesus was teaching in church. A woman who had been plagued with an infirmity for 18 years was in church that day. The Bible does not tell us what this infirmity was. Whatever the infirmity, it caused the woman to be unable to lift herself; God attributes her infirmity to Satan. However, this infirmity did not stop the woman from being in church on the Sabbath day.

Jesus called the woman to Him. He said, "...Woman, thou art loosed from thine infirmity." He laid His hands upon her, and the Bible says that she was made straight. She gave the glory to God.

The ruler of the synagogue criticized Jesus for healing on the Sabbath day. He made comment that Jesus had six other days to heal. Why did He have to heal her on the Sabbath day?

Jesus called the ruler a hypocrite. Jesus pointed out that many Jews loosed their ox or ass from the stall and led them to the watering trough on the Sabbath day. Should not this woman who had been bound by Satan for 18 years be healed on the Sabbath Day? When Jesus said this, His adversaries were ashamed, but his friends rejoiced.

Reading this story has caused me to be reminded of the redeeming power of Jesus Christ. Recently I counseled with a girl who had been involved in some very serious sin. Though she is a girl who lives in a distant state and with whom I have not spent very much time, I consider her to be my friend; I love her. This girl recounted to me a life of sin and then shared with me how God had recently begun to change her life.

BLESSED REDEEMER

There are times in our lives when a word or an idea which we have heard all of our lives suddenly becomes more real and meaningful than it has ever been before. Such is the case of the word *Redeemer* in my life recently.

Because I have a wonderful Christian heritage and wonderful Christian parents, I have heard the word *Redeemer* spoken often, probably before I was old enough to even remember. I have sung and heard songs like "Blessed Redeemer" since I was just a little girl. And though I have grown to love such songs and the Redeemer about whom they are written, I must admit that the word *Redeemer* had little personal meaning. At least, I did not thrill when I heard the sound of it…until this week.

I am such a sheltered person (Praise the Lord!) that never before have I been close to someone who has suffered in their life the awfulness of sin quite like the friend with whom I talked this week. At least I didn't realize it…until this week. Since talking with this friend— learning what she has been through and how much she has changed— the Holy Spirit keeps whispering in my ear and in my heart the word *Redeemer*. And I am grateful for His message.

The sweet Holy Spirit keeps whispering the words of Psalm 103:4a which says, *"Who redeemeth thy life from destruction."* This is a verse I have read several times from my youth but it had little significance for me. But this week Psalm 103:4 has found a new resting place in the depths of my heart.

My friend shared with me that she was involved in things which almost led to her destruction. I shudder just to think of how close that destruction came. But then she turned to the Redeemer, and she has been reclaimed to usefulness. The Lord surely has used her testimony in my life.

Just in case you know of someone or if you are someone who needs his or her life redeemed, just in case you are a wife and mother who recognizes your need for the Redeemer to create usefulness in your life or in the lives of your family, allow me to share with you some lessons from a woman who was loosed (or redeemed) from her infirmity.

1 **If you want to see redemption, you must be faithful to God's house.** This is where my friend's destruction began. She quit attending the house of God. Church, after all, was a waste of time. There are so many hypocrites there. But the woman in this story came to church though she could not even lift herself. Perhaps she recognized that the house of God is where the work of redemption takes place. Church is where we hear the preaching of the Word of God. Preaching is the foolish and yet powerful tool God has chosen with which to work His plan of redemption.

If you want your family to be redeemed into usefulness for Him, teach them to be faithful to the house of God. And teach them not to critique while they are there, but rather to seek help and strength as the woman in this story did.

2 **If you want to see redemption, you must pray for others.** In this story the woman did not seek Jesus; He sought her. Though it is true that this woman was in the right place at the right time, she did not ask Jesus to heal her, but rather Jesus called for her. I wonder if, perhaps, someone else was praying and asking Jesus for her.

I have a list of people I know have wandered from the Lord. I pray for them often. I often ask the Lord to watch out for them and to stay close to them even though they may not have the spiritual strength to ask this for themselves.

Sometimes, the Lord wakes me in the middle of the night. I often ask Him when I awake, for whom He wants me to pray. He often puts in my mind the name or the face of a person whom I know to be very far from Him. I get up, go to the easy chair in my living room, and I kneel to pray for that person. The person may not be asking God for His help, but I believe that someday Jesus will call that person, and He will redeem him to usefulness again.

I wonder who carried the woman to church. She could not have attended on her own. Someone must have aided her. Perhaps this woman did not want to attend church, but someone talked her into it. May I ask you, "Are you encouraging anyone to attend church? Do you knock on anyone's door to invite him? Are you discouraged when that person hides from you as he sees you coming to his door or when you must talk him into coming week after week?" Do not be discouraged! I have seen Jesus finally call many folks like this, and I have seen them redeemed.

May I ask you, "Do you intercede with God on the behalf of anyone who needs to be redeemed? Are you tempted to give up as you see their lives go from bad to worse?" Don't give up! The Redeemer will come! Wives and mothers, are you pleading with the Redeemer on behalf of your husband and children? You may say, "They are good people; they don't need to be redeemed." May I remind you that in order to be useful, we all must be touched by the Blessed Redeemer. You and I need to be redeemed!

(3) **If you want to see redemption, you must put more emphasis on people than on tradition.** When Jesus saw the woman, He wasn't concerned with His laws concerning the Sabbath. He cared too much about this woman's soul.

Many church members are easily offended by non-traditional methods and by non-traditional people. They are just not accustomed to gang-type people coming to their church. They are used to attending church with those who are already saved and sanctified. This explains why they rarely get to see the work of redemption in their churches.

Many wives and mothers are too busy living their traditional lives to be interested in being creative in their approach to inspiring their loved ones toward redemption. When my children were just babies, I often sang to them about salvation. I would come home from teaching a hundred or so college girls, and I would sit my baby on his changing table where I would teach him and sing to him as if he understood every word. I often prayed, as I made the transition from being a "college professor" to "just a mother," that I would remember that the latter job was much more important.

I have seen my husband do crazy non-traditional things in order to teach our children. I have sometimes wondered why he had to act so childish and then later wondered why they listened to his words of admonition so much better than mine.

If you want to see God redeem a life, you must value that life more than tradition. You must value that soul more than anything—more than your business, your schedule, your living room sofa—more than anything.

It is hard for me to believe that the Pharisees cared more about the Sabbath than they did about seeing Jesus perform a miracle of redemption. But they did. Many unsaved people who live in the world care more about humpbacked whales than they do about the dying souls of aborted children. And many Christians are just as guilty, for they care more about their traditions than they do about those whom Jesus wants to redeem.

4 **If you want to see redemption, you must rejoice and give glory to God!** When Jesus healed the woman, His *"...adversaries were ashamed: and all the people rejoiced for all the glorious things that were done by him."* (Luke 13:17) My emotions have been mixed this week: I have been filled with sorrow over the near destructive sin which enveloped the life of my friend; yet I have wanted to shout and to praise the Lord for the glorious redemption which He has performed in her life. To be honest, I have had a difficult time deciding what to do most—sorrow or rejoice. And my emotions have also been gripped with fear. What if my friend turns back to her sin?

Now I have decided what my emotion will be. I WILL REJOICE! I will trust the Lord that His redemption will be complete. I will trust Him to continue to call for my friend and to work in her life. And I will praise Him because He has redeemed my friend from destruction and not only has He redeemed her life—but He has also redeemed yours and mine.

Blessed Redeemer! Precious Redeemer!
Seems now I see Him on Calvary's tree;

BLESSED REDEEMER

Wounded and bleeding, for sinners pleading—
Blind and unheeding—dying for me.

"Dear Lord,
     You died to redeem my friend—and me. I WILL REJOICE!
Amen."

Distracted

A Lesson From Mary and Martha
Part I

"And Jesus answered and said unto her, Martha, Martha,
thou art careful and troubled about many things:
But one thing is needful: and Mary hath chosen that good part,
which shall not be taken away from her."
(Luke 10:41, 42)

Chapter 13
Mary and Martha, Part 1
Luke 10:38-42

WHILE FLYING TO Santa Clara, California, with my husband to speak at a marriage seminar, I asked my husband this question, "If you were to speak to the ladies at this seminar, what do you think would be the most important thing to teach them?"

He answered, "I believe that the most important concept you could teach a group of married ladies is how to have a consistently happy spirit." I believe the following story contains some helps on how to have that kind of a spirit, and I have used it to teach this many times to many ladies.

In Luke chapter 10, we read the story of a woman named Martha who received Jesus into her home. Martha had a sister named Mary who sat at Jesus' feet and heard His Word. The Bible tells us that Martha was "...*cumbered about much serving....*" Because Martha was cumbered, she began to complain to the Lord and to criticize her sister Mary for her lack of service. Martha began to cry out for help.

As a wife and mother, I can relate to Martha's feelings and to her tactics. There have been times when I also was "...*cumbered about much serving....*" What woman hasn't at some time in her life sought out her other family members to plead for their help in the kitchen? I am afraid that I have sometimes been tempted to close (or should I say, "slam") the cabinet doors a little more loudly than usual or to be a little extra rough with the dishes as a signal to my family that I do not appreciate their lack of service in the kitchen. I find that I feel a little sorry for myself. I may even feel a bit critical of them for choosing to do something else in the house rather than opting to help their overworked wife and mother. What I am trying to say is that I understand Martha's feeling all too well. In fact, I am tempted to take her side in the entire matter.

I am tempted to take Martha's side in the quarrel until I read Jesus' response to Martha in Luke 10:41 and 42. Jesus tells Martha that she is *"...careful and troubled about many things."* Jesus says, *"But one thing is needful: and Mary hath chosen that good part, which shall not be taken away from her."* In other words, while I am tempted to take Martha's side in the dispute, Jesus takes the side of Mary. However, as I have studied and taken apart this story piece by piece, I find myself not only on the side of Mary, but also on the side of Jesus as well—which is always the only safe place to be. Allow me to share with you the lessons I found from God's Word which brought me to the **right** side of this matter.

(**1**) **Jesus is not saying that we must always sit at His feet in order to please Him.** This had always been what confused me about the story. Why was Jesus not pleased with Martha when she was probably busy preparing a meal for Him? Are we not to serve Jesus? Are we to sit at His feet **all** of the time? Are people who sit at Jesus' feet really more spiritual and pleasing to the Lord than those who are busily serving Him?

No, Jesus was not rebuking Martha for being busy serving Him. Rather, He was rebuking her for being *"cumbered"* while serving. The word *cumbered* means "distracted." If Jesus was disappointed in Martha, it was because while she was serving Him, she had forgotten Whom she was serving. She had become distracted. In doing so, her spirit had become wounded.

I find in my own life a tendency to become distracted by many things even while I am serving the Lord. When I allow the following things to distract me from the Lord, I struggle with an unhappy spirit.

A. *Money.* I find sometimes as I am busily serving the Lord and my family, I become distracted by money. That is, I begin to worry about where money will come for different needs that I have. Before I know it, my mind and my heart are distracted from the Lord and from the blessings of my time spent "at His feet" in devotions that morning. When I realized that money had often distracted me from the Lord and His Word, I made myself this promise. I promised that I would not allow myself to think about money as I served the Lord and my family. Rather, I would only think about money at a time that I had previously set aside for the paying of bills, balancing of the checkbook, or for the establishing of the budget, etc. (Though my husband pays the bills in our family, I have a separate checking account for my allowance, and I pay a few bills from that account.) I would not allow my mind to wander to thoughts about money at an unplanned time. Money can quickly distract us from the Lord even as we are serving Him.

A few years ago my husband began to give me a generous allowance every two weeks. The first several months that I received this allowance, I found myself going over and over in my mind how I was going to spend this allowance. I would try to figure how I was going to save a few pennies in one area so that I could spend a few more in another area. Before I knew it, I had been distracted from the Lord, and my spirit was often depressed. As soon as I was aware of what had happened, I established a set time for dividing my allowance. Then I promised myself that I would never again spend unplanned time thinking about money.

B. *Possessions.* Thinking about possessions is another way that we are often distracted from the Lord. For example, I keep a list of things that I need to purchase for my home. It often seems that the list gets longer instead of shorter. My spirit becomes distracted by worry. If I worry about the needs I have or about the possessions I desire to have, I find that I am carnal in my spirit and I am distracted from spiritual things. Because of this, I keep a list of things I need, and I bring them before the Lord in prayer. I may purchase them as the Lord supplies the money, but I do not spend unplanned time worrying or desiring earthly possessions.

C. *Problems.* Problems are another thing which "cumber" us about much serving and distract us from the One Whom makes our spirits joyful. When I first started doing some marriage counseling, I often found myself distracted from the Lord as I took those marriage problems home with me. I carried them around with me as I served the Lord and others. I have learned to take these marriages to the Lord and not to spend unscheduled time worrying about them. Instead, I spend my time dwelling upon the promises of the Lord. I also dwell upon the faith I have that God can bless my own marriage.

I believe that Christians tend to think that they must constantly be burdened about their unsaved or backslidden loved ones in order to see them saved or brought back to the Lord. I find that the opposite is true. When I dwell on the problems of my loved ones, I am distracted from the Lord and too spiritually depressed to be a help to anyone. Because of this, I take the problems of my loved ones to the Lord in prayer each day, and I **leave** those problems with Him. I choose to help my loved ones with their varied problems by doing kind deeds for them, speaking kind words to them and, most of all, by praying for them. I do **not** choose to help them by worrying about them, thereby distracting myself from the One Whom we all need the most.

D. *Mindless tasks.* I find that after I have had my daily devotions, I feel extremely close to my Lord. It is my firm belief that daily time of **just** sitting at Jesus' feet and hearing His Word **is** very important. However, Jesus is also pleased when we do the daily tasks of service to the Lord and to others. Jesus wants us to read our Bibles and pray, but He is also pleased when we do the things necessary to have a clean house.

So many of the tasks that must be done in order to keep a house clean are boring and mindless and therefore do nothing to feed our spirits. If we do not plan what to think about as we do these chores, we will find ourselves distracted from the Lord at the end of a day of housekeeping, and we will greet our families with an unpleasant spirit. I fight this tendency to be distracted from the Lord as I do mindless tasks by listening to sermon tapes as I go about my housework and other chores.

Some women believe that their lot in life is inferior to that of the man's because a housewife's life is full of so many tasks that take very little thinking and creativity. However, it is these tasks for which I may be the most grateful. It is when I am doing the mindless tasks that I have the most opportunity to put my mind upon the Lord.

I am trying to say that service is important! Though God does wish us to spend devotional time at His feet hearing His Word, He is also pleased when we serve Him. However, as we serve Him, we do not have to be distracted. We can find ways to keep our minds constantly upon the One Whom we serve.

The same thought can be applied to a marriage. Many wives get so caught up in the distractions of child rearing, housework, problems and materialism that they rarely even think about the husband whom they are serving. I listen to a lot of tapes on marriage and avoid spending too much time worrying about the previously mentioned things so that I will not be distracted from my love for my husband and so that I will have a happy spirit to share with him.

(2) **We can usually tell when we have become distracted.** People who are distracted have spirits that are negative and critical. Because Martha was distracted, she complained about having to serve alone. She was critical of her sister's choice to sit at Jesus' feet.

There have been times in my own life when I was critical of the woman who I felt did not **do** enough for the Lord. At other times, I have found myself critical of the woman who I thought did too much and neglected her home and family. Whenever I find myself being critical of the schedules of others, I do not reveal my own good spiritual judgment; rather, I reveal that I have been distracted from the Lord and that I possess a bad spirit.

Jesus told Martha that she was careful and troubled about many things. The word *careful* means "anxious," and the word *troubled* means "disturbed." Another sign of distraction from the Lord is a spirit that is plagued by worry. When we are distracted from the Lord, we will be anxious and disturbed about the cares of this world.

3 **Though Jesus is pleased with our service, it is our attention to Him and to His Word which is most needful in our lives.** The word *needful* means "to edify" or "build up." It is our attention to the Lord which builds our spirits as Christians. Our attention to the Lord is the **only** thing which is needful in our lives. When we serve the Lord with the wrong motive, when our attention is not upon our love for Him, we have been distracted from the **only** thing which is needful for our spirits.

4 **It is our time with and our love for the Lord which cannot be taken away from us.** The things which would distract us from the Lord—such as money, possessions, loved ones, and chores—can all be taken away from us. We may lose our money and our home with its possessions. A loved one may pass away or even betray us. We may lose the strength to fulfill the tasks of housework or the Lord's work. Yet our Lord will go with us wherever we may go. He cannot be taken away from us. The things from His Word which we store in our hearts cannot be removed from us either. We will always have our love for the Lord while we live on this earth, and we will be able to love Him for all eternity. How great of our Lord to have put Martha's mind upon the one thing which could not be taken away from her—the one thing which could keep her spirit consistently happy. How I have learned to love the story of Mary and Martha and the lesson learned therein. *"...and that ye may attend upon the Lord without distraction."* (I Corinthians 7:35b)

Practical Lessons on Keeping a Happy Spirit

1. Play sermon tapes when doing mindless tasks.
2. Listen to **praise** music, especially when doing mundane tasks

such as cleaning the house or driving a car. Avoid listening to even Christian music which creates a melancholy spirit of self-pity.

3. Make friends with someone who makes you laugh. I have a friend whom I made a habit of calling during an especially difficult time just because she makes me laugh.

4. Go outdoors. Fresh air freshens our spirit, and nature brings us closer to God.

5. Exercise and maintain your vitality. Exercise is one of those things which depresses our spirits before we do it and strongly encourages our spirits afterwards. Avoid that which would have the opposite effect such as overeating. Always remember that your husband is your first priority. If you have served the Lord all day but you have the spirit of a wet dish rag when he arrives home, your priorities have become confused.

6. Intersperse work and play. Reward yourself for your hard work and accomplishments during the day.

7. Nap. This will help your spirit to still be strong during the evening hours which is the time of day when women see their families the most.

8. Eat right. Take vitamins.

9. Read uplifting books.

10. Avoid entertainment which will leave you with a depressed spirit such as romance novels, catalogs (which show a lot of things we can't afford), magazines, television (talk shows, soap operas and even the news), worldly radio and gossip. *Sermon ended!*

11. Be a consistent soul winner, both at scheduled times and at spontaneous times. There is nothing more uplifting to the spirit than winning a soul to Christ.

12. Spend time for others visiting nursing homes, hospitals and visiting those who are in need.

13. Schedule daily conversational time for immediate family and, perhaps, weekly times for extended family members.

"Dear Lord,
   Please help me to keep a happy spirit so that I will keep from becoming distracted. Amen."

The Other Side of the Story

A Lesson From Mary and Martha
Part II

"Now Jesus loved Martha,
and her sister, and Lazarus."
(John 11:5)

Chapter 14
Mary and Martha, Part 2
John 11

*I*N JOHN 11, WE have another side to the story of Mary and Martha. That same zealous personality which distracted Martha from sitting at Jesus' feet in Luke 10 served Martha well in the story in John.

Lazarus was sick, and the two sisters sent someone to tell Jesus about it. Two days after Jesus had heard the news, He announced to His disciples that He was going to return to Judæa. Not too long before this, the Saviour had left Judæa with His disciples because the Jews sought to stone Him. The disciples questioned Jesus' wisdom in returning to the same place. It is sweet to me that Jesus was willing to go back and face the Jews because, as is stated in verse 5, *"Now Jesus loved Martha, and her sister, and Lazarus."*

It is especially sweet to me to see Jesus mentioning Martha's name first. Martha was the one who did **not** sit at Jesus' feet when He visited her home. Martha had been the critical, worried, and distracted one in this instance. She had been the one who had **not** chosen the good part. It was Martha whom Jesus had to rebuke. Yet He mentions Martha's name first and, in this instance, does not mention Mary's name at all. He goes to Judæa and faces grave danger because He loves this family, and He loves Martha first of all. How wonderful to know that Christ loves us even, and perhaps especially, when He has to rebuke us. He loves us though we may be distracted, critical, worried, and far from Him.

I believe that Jesus loved Martha because He understood the assets and the liabilities of her personality though it was very different from her sister's. The diligence to get the job done shows again in Martha's personality in John 11, for it was Martha who met Jesus as soon as she heard that He was coming. Mary, however, sat still in the house. Why? Perhaps Mary's less bold personality caused her to grieve so for her brother that she was unable to move to action as her sister did. The Bible tells us that there were many people comforting Mary while Martha ran for help. Perhaps Mary had the extra faith to understand that Jesus could hear her plea even while she sat still in the house. Regardless of the reason, it was Martha who again showed herself the more aggressive as she ran to meet Jesus.

In this account, it is Martha's turn to shine as she expresses her faith in the Lord. She said, "...Lord, if thou hadst been here, my brother had not died." Then she makes a statement which has become one of my favorite verses in the Bible. "But I know, that even now, whatsoever thou wilt ask of God, God will give it thee." (John 11:22)

The Bible is sweet to show us not only Martha's faith, but also the smallness and the vulnerability of that faith. Jesus told Martha that Lazarus would rise again. Martha expressed her confidence that Lazarus would rise again at the last day, but she did seem to have had her doubts that Lazarus would actually be brought to life before her that very day. This seems quite contradictory to the faith she expressed in verse 22.

This reminds me of my own faith. One minute, I believe God can do anything and that He **will** answer my prayer. The next minute, I am worrying about the future as if there were no God at all. Yet God over-looks the faithlessness of both Martha and myself and reacts to the faith that we **do** have.

I don't believe it was Martha's **great** faith which caused her to see her brother raised from the dead. I think that Martha saw this miracle because she did two things:

- She put the little bit of faith that she **did** have to action by sending for Jesus and by running to meet Him.

- She expressed the faith that she had by saying to Jesus such things as, "*Yea, Lord: I believe that thou art the Christ, the Son of God, which should come into the world.*" I make it a practice in my prayer time not only to ask God to answer my prayers, but also to express my belief to God that He will answer my prayers. My faith is certainly not great, but I express what faith I do have to Jesus.

The next thing Martha did was run to Mary and bring her to Jesus. She told Mary, "*...The Master is come, and calleth for thee.*" Martha uses what is to me one of the sweetest words that can be used when speaking to Jesus: "*Master.*" As soon as Mary heard the message, she arose quickly and went to Jesus. How sweet that God used Mary's less aggressive personality in Luke chapter 10 to teach Martha a valuable lesson! It is also sweet that God used Martha and her opposite type of personality to bring her sister to Jesus in John chapter 11.

Mary fell at Jesus' feet and wept when she saw Him. Her grief caused Jesus to weep with her. How marvelous to realize that Jesus weeps with us when we weep. When Jesus saw the dead body of His beloved Lazarus, He wept again. All the Jews who watched Jesus recognized the greatness of Jesus' love for Lazarus.

Jesus' tears moved Him to action, and He asked that the stone be removed which was on Lazarus' grave. Martha, the fastidious housekeeper, still did not have enough faith to understand what was about to happen. Instead, like a typical female, she was most concerned about the smell. Jesus tried to strengthen Martha's faith by saying, "*...Said I not unto thee, that, if thou wouldest believe, thou shouldest see the glory of God?*"

Jesus thanked the Father for His answer to prayer in advance so that all those watching would understand and believe. Then He cried, "*...Lazarus, come forth.*" Lazarus came forth bound in grave clothes. Jesus said, "*...Loose him, and let him go.*" John 11:45 tells us that many were saved because of witnessing Lazarus' resurrection from the dead.

This story is so full of good and sweet lessons and truths, most of which I have already mentioned, but I want to simplify and capsulize the lessons I have found here.

(1) **We should be patient with the liabilities and appreciate the assets of our personalities and the personalities of others.** We should not use our personality weaknesses as excuses to keep us from being **all** that we should be for the Lord. Yet we should remember that God loves us and can use us in spite of the fact that we may be different from someone else. We should be patient with those who are different from ourselves.

(2) **We should remember that God loves us in spite of, and perhaps because of, our personality weaknesses.** Jesus illustrates this beautifully by emphasizing His love for Martha rather than Mary in this story.

(3) **We should not be discouraged when our faith is weak.** We can see several times in this Biblical account the smallness of Martha's faith. Yet God performed one of His most notable miracles for her.

(4) **We should allow our faith, even though it is small, to move us to action.** We should actively seek the Lord in our grief. We should express what faith we *do* have to the Lord.

(5) **We should realize that Jesus can use us, in spite of our personality weaknesses, to bring others to Him.** It was Martha who was the weaker Christian in Luke, chapter 10. But it was Mary who needed a Martha to meet Jesus and bring her to Him in John, chapter 11. Martha's diligent nature caused her to have a part in many Jews' salvation after they witnessed the resurrection of Lazarus from the dead.

6 **We should make Jesus our Master and come to Him as soon as He calls us.** *"And when she had so said, she went her way, and called Mary her sister secretly, saying, The Master is come, and calleth for thee. As soon as she heard that, she arose quickly, and came unto him."* (John 11:28, 29)

7 **We should realize that Jesus weeps with us when we weep.** I am not sure that Jesus weeps with us every time we weep, but that's a wonderful thought—and perhaps He does! Yet, I learn in John 11 that there **is** definitely a time when Jesus weeps with His children. Perhaps it is in the death of a loved one. Perhaps it is **every** time we weep. There is a time when God weeps with His children, and He notices each falling tear.

So, here we have two completely different stories about two completely different sisters and their unique strengths and weaknesses. I am reminded today about how much God loves each one of my sisters in Christ and how He uses us and loves us in spite of our differences. May we be patient with all those sisters in Christ who are different from us, and may we love them also.

She Left Her Waterpot

A Lesson From
the Woman at the Well

"Jesus answered and said unto her,
Whosoever drinketh of this water shall thirst again:
But whosoever drinketh of the water
that I shall give him shall never thirst."
(John 4:13, 14a)

Chapter 15
The Woman at the Well
John 4:3 - 30

*J*MUST ADMIT THAT I am what you could call an absent-minded person. Because I teach part-time at Hyles-Anderson College, I refer to myself as the "absent-minded professor." I think the professor part just helps me to feel a little bit better about my absent-mindedness!

When I was growing up in the Hyles household, my mother was always having to remind me of this and that, and sometimes she would even say (lovingly, of course), "Cindy, you would forget your head if it wasn't attached."

God must surely have a sense of humor, because He gave me a daughter who remembers much better than I do. Sometimes she reminds me not to forget my keys before I lock the door, etc. I think things are sort of turned around in our household, but I am thankful that God has always made sure that there is someone around to help me to remember.

Perhaps it is my absent-mindedness which drew my attention to a certain phrase in John, chapter 4. I was reading the story about the woman at the well. Many details about this story capture my attention. First of all, I love the fact that Jesus was tired and thus "plopped" Himself down in kind of an uncomfortable place on the side of a well. (I wonder if the cultured people passing by wondered why He was sitting there?) I love the fact that a woman from the "enemy" race approached Him and that Jesus was the first to strike up a friendly conversation. I love His humble Spirit in that He not only talked to this

She Left Her Waterpot

heathen lady, but He also asked her for a drink of water. I love the way Jesus promised this lady a drink which would cause her to never thirst again. It is exciting to read about this lady's salvation and about the many other Samaritans who were also saved.

Yet, my favorite part of this wonderful story are the words: *"The woman then left her waterpot...."* It doesn't seem that she meant to leave it. It seems that she got so excited about other things that she just forgot it was there. (I've done that before, have you?)

At one point in my life, I had a waterpot of my own which I was carrying around with me. With that waterpot, I was trying to quench my own thirst for satisfaction and for self-esteem. As I got closer to Jesus, I was confronted with the fact that I was trying to quench my thirst with the wrong things. I found in my waterpot vanity and pride and a desire for man's approval. I had tried to quench my thirst with these and with other tangibles in my waterpot such as money, material possessions, and even food. I even found relationships in my waterpot.

I came face to face with the fact that many of the things in my waterpot were not really sinful; it was just that I had been using them for the wrong purpose. God seemed to say, "Cindy, anytime a woman tries to find satisfaction in anything other than Me, that is sin." I was ashamed and desperately wanted to let go of my waterpot, but I had, after all, been carrying it around with me for a very long time. I was afraid to part with it.

I suppose that is why I was so blessed when I came across those words again recently, *"The woman then left her waterpot...."* For suddenly, it dawned on me that I, too, had left mine. I didn't really mean to leave it, but I just got so excited about other things that I forgot it was there. I realized that God had delivered me in a large measure from trying to find satisfaction in the wrong things. The following are some reasons why I believe I left my waterpot.

1. **I realized that it is a sin to try to find satisfaction, comfort or self-esteem in anything other than my relationship with Jesus and His Word.** The following are some examples of these.

I suppose at some time I have tried to find satisfaction in all of them. But they only satisfied for a while. They quenched my thirst for self-esteem or comfort for a while, and then I found my thirst for these things to be greater than ever. You might say that these were addicting rather than satisfying.

- Money, often via the use of credit cards

- Possessions, such as things for the house or clothing

- Appearance, which is an area where many women are tempted to find their self-esteem.

- Popularity

- Relationships, such as the marriage relationship, the parent/child relationship, and when I was younger, even the boyfriend/girlfriend relationship.

- Food (yes, even food) which causes many to struggle with their weight because of trying to find in food what should come from a relationship with the Holy Spirit—comfort. This is not always the reason for weight problems, but oftentimes it is.

(2) **I began to seek a stronger relationship with Jesus and found in Him the things for which I was really longing.** I really think that increasing my time in the Bible, prayer, and in service for Christ helped me more than anything else to "leave my waterpot." I began doing several practical things that helped me spend more time with the Lord. Perhaps some of these ideas will work for you.

A. One morning a week in place of my regular devotions, I began doing intensive Bible study. It is from these studies that my two books on Bible women have developed—*Silk and Purple* and *A Meek and Quiet Spirit.*

B. I began praying in the car and while doing daily chores, **as well as** at my regularly scheduled devotion time.

C. I began to sing and to praise God more.

D. I began to listen to at least one sermon tape a day when I had most of the day to spend at home.

E. I began memorizing large portions of Scripture. I learn two new verses in my devotions each day and review four verses which I have already memorized. I have now memorized the verses in most of the books in the New Testament.

F. I started again to yield myself to the Holy Spirit several times a day while asking for forgiveness of sin.

G. I drastically decreased my intake of worldly entertainments and influences such as television, worldly radio shows, etc.

3 **I began to resist the impulse to make myself feel better by indulging in the wrong things.** I did not stop buying clothes and things for my house. Rather, I stopped buying them when my self-esteem was low in order to cure that problem. I stopped doing things that were bad for me in order to enhance my appearance. This would be good advice for the "sun worshiper" or for the person who starves herself of nutrition in order to be thin.

I did not stop eating (and, unfortunately, I did not stop overeating altogether). But I did admit that gluttony is a sin, and I began to make this a matter of prayer in my life. I began to resist overeating when I was depressed in order to find comfort. I did not stop trying to improve my relationships or to please others, but I quit looking for others' approval to give me satisfaction and self-esteem. I learned to react to depression by putting more of Christ into my life.

4 **I began to share more of Christ with others.** I have increased the amount of time that I spend sharing Christ with others. As I have shared Him in soul winning, I have realized that I already have what I need to satisfy me. I recognize it as flowing out of me, not only as I witness to others, but also as I minister to others with visits to nursing homes, hospitals, and in other ways. I really do find satisfaction not with what I put in, which comes from the waterpot, but rather with what I bring out from the Holy Spirit Who lives within me.

This reminds me of a favorite Christian chorus:

> I've got a river of life flowing out of me,
> Makes the lame to walk and the blind to see,
> Opens prison doors, sets the captives free;
> I've got a river of life flowing out of me.
> Spring up, oh well, within my soul.
> Spring up, oh well, and make me whole.
> Spring up, oh well, till all may see
> Your life abundantly.

(5) I began to have faith in the end results of sharing Christ with others. The Bible tells us that Jesus tarried with the Samaritans two more days after the woman at the well was saved, and many others were saved also. The woman found satisfaction in Christ, and that satisfaction was used in the lives of many others. What this remarkable woman may not know is that her testimony was used in my life just recently. What a miracle that one woman's sharing of Christ can be used thousands of years later!

I came to a point when I decided to believe that God can do great things with me every time I open my mouth, even and perhaps especially when I don't see it. It will be exciting to get to Heaven and find out what great things He has done in response to our faith. It is tremendously exciting today just to have the opportunity to share Him with others.

So you see, somewhere along the line, I very absent-mindedly left my waterpot. I didn't really mean to leave it; I wasn't strong enough to let go on my own. I just got so excited about other things that I forgot it was there. If I think really hard, I might figure out where I left it, but I'm not sure when I left it. I suppose there will be days I'll be tempted to go back and get it...but I don't think I will. You see, I haven't really missed it at all!

Reacting Properly to Sin

A Lesson From
the Woman Taken in Adultery

"If we confess our sins,
he is faithful and just to forgive us our sins,
and to cleanse us from all unrighteousness."
(I John 1:9)

Chapter 16
The Woman Taken in Adultery
John 8:1 - 11

The points in this chapter were taken from a sermon preached by Dr. Jack Schaap. (Used by permission)

IN JOHN 8:1-11, Jesus sets forth for us a perfect example of the proper way to react to the sins of others. The story begins with Jesus going to the Mount of Olives, probably to rest and to pray. Early in the morning, He went to the temple, and the Bible says *"and all the people came unto him; and he sat down, and taught them."* (John 8:2b)

While Jesus was teaching, the scribes and Pharisees brought to Him a woman whom they had actually found in the act of adultery. They had witnessed it, and they were sure that it was true. Theirs was not just an example of proper reaction to gossip, but to legitimate sin.

The penalty for adultery at this time was death. The scribes and Pharisees asked if this woman should be stoned for her sin. They asked this question in order to tempt Christ. They were hypocritical in their concern about this woman's sin. In fact, though they called Jesus their Master, they had called Him a deceiver just the day before. (Read the account in John 7:40-53.)

When the scribes and Pharisees accused the woman and questioned Jesus, He did not answer immediately. Instead, Jesus stooped down and with his finger wrote on the ground. It was a long time before Jesus spoke. When He did, He said, *"He that is without sin among you, let him first cast a stone at her."* (John 8:7b) And again, Jesus stooped down and wrote on the ground.

Those who had accused this woman were convicted, and they departed one by one until Jesus was left alone with the woman. In John

REACTING PROPERLY TO SIN

8:10b Jesus asked, *"Woman, where are those thine accusers? hath no man condemned thee?"*

She answered in verse 11, *"...No man, Lord...."*

"And Jesus said unto her, Neither do I condemn thee: go, and sin no more." (John 8:11b)

I would like to point out from this story some lessons about how to react to the sins of others. Because this is a book which is primarily directed toward wives and mothers, I would also like to point out from this story lessons about how to react to the weaknesses of our husbands and of our children.

(1) **In order to react properly to the sins and weaknesses of others, one must get alone and have a daily time of prayer with the Lord.** Notice in John 8:1 that Jesus had been to the Mount of Olives before He went to teach in the temple. The Mount of Olives was a favorite prayer place of the Saviour. Jesus often departed alone to a quiet place before He taught the multitudes.

So many times when I have felt confused about how to deal with the sins of others in my counseling, etc., I have found complete peace about the situation after spending time alone in prayer, seeking God's help in the matter. In the Christian wife course which I teach at Hyles-Anderson College, the students and I discuss how to communicate when there are problems in a marriage. The first step I give them is this: Pray about it for at least 24 hours.

It takes much self-control to wait and to pray about a problem before discussing it, especially when angry. But praying first helps us to avoid saying things we should not. It also helps to avoid the temptation to discuss problems at times and in places where it would be embarrassing and inappropriate.

Many times after seeking the Lord's face, I realize that a certain problem does not need to be discussed. Sometimes, however, God does give me peace about discussing it with the person involved. He also gives me the right attitude, the right timing, and the right plan for communicating the problem.

2 In order to react properly to the sins and weaknesses of others, one must be a student and a teacher of God's Word. Jesus was busy teaching God's Word when He reacted properly to sin. Prayer and Bible study not only give us wisdom about how to deal with the weaknesses and sins of others, but they also humble us as they convict us of our own sin. Proud, arrogant and condemning Christians are probably not praying Christians who are living in the Bible.

Teaching God's Word also helps us to have the right attitude toward sin. When one is winning souls to Christ and discipling those baby Christians, he is more patient and compassionate toward sin.

3 In order to react properly to the sins and weaknesses of others, one must stay in church. Jesus was in the temple when He reacted properly to sin. One who is faithful to church is less likely to be a Pharisee than one who is not. The world is full of Pharisees who mow the grass and go fishing on Sundays because the church, they say, is full of hypocrites. These Pharisees would be better off spiritually if they would listen to that imperfect preacher and become convicted of their own sins rather than just of the sins of others.

4 In order to react properly to the sins and weaknesses of others, do not respond right away to accusations. If you hear that someone you know has sinned, there is no need to get on the phone and tell your best friend what you think. If you hear that someone has said or done something against you, there is no need to confront that person and to lose your temper right away. If you find weakness in your husband or children, there is no need to point out that weakness right away.

As a teacher, I would never confront a student immediately or spontaneously about a problem he is having in class. To stop a student in the hallway "on the spur of the moment" and to criticize that student for a weakness shows tremendous disrespect. If I must criticize or be negative to a student, I owe that person the courtesy to make an appointment and to plan how I will discuss the problem.

If I owe this kind of courtesy to my students and if Jesus showed this kind of courtesy to an adulterer, surely we should show this kind of courtesy to our husbands and to our children. Wait and plan before you point out a weakness to your loved ones.

5 **In order to react properly to the sins and weaknesses of others, one must identify with the sinner.** Why did Jesus stoop down and write on the ground? First, He humbled Himself before this sinner by positioning Himself to be lower than she. Secondly, He wrote on the dirt, I believe, to remind His listeners of that from which we are all made: dirt.

I have spoken and written on some pretty convicting topics in my classes and in my books. Yet people often respond favorably to some of the most convicting messages. Why? First, because of the Lord and His mercy in allowing me to be used of Him. Secondly, because I try to identify with others by admitting my own weaknesses. I often try to speak and write as if I am only correcting my own weakness and allowing others to listen in as I do so. In the process, people find in my teachings their own weaknesses and also a way to correct them, without feeling threatened by the one who has pointed them out.

I strive to handle my children the same way also. Often when they come to me with some temptation they are facing, I relate to them by sharing a similar struggle I have had in my own life.

And though I rarely feel it is my duty to point out a weakness to my spouse (Have I mentioned to you that he is almost perfect?!), if I must discuss a problem with him, I never place the blame completely on him. All of the blame is too heavy for any person to have placed upon him. Even the best of people will respond defensively if they find themselves backed into a corner with no way of escape. After you discuss a problem with your loved one, you should leave them with self-respect.

6 **In order to react properly to the sins and weaknesses of others, one should ignore many accusations.** Of course, because I am involved in the ministry of a large church as well as a large college, there could be many opportunities to hear accusations such as the following:

- "Susie doesn't like you. She said something bad about you."

- "Susie doesn't like Mary. Did you hear what she said about her?"

- "Did you hear that Susie is seeing Mary's husband?"

- "Susie just does not have our standards."

- "Susie is not loyal to our church."

- "I don't think Susie is a fundamentalist."

The fact that my husband and I sometimes travel and work by phone with people all over our country and, to a certain extent, all over the world, gives us an opportunity to hear even more accusations. Proverbs 26:17 says, *"He that passeth by, and meddleth with strife belonging not to him, is like one that taketh a dog by the ears."*

I have a new floppy-eared puppy who loves to bite, so I can imagine what injury would come to me should I grab her by the ears. To meddle with strife which is none of my business will also cause me injury.

Because of this, I avoid listening to gossip if at all possible. When I do hear gossip, I try to ignore it. If the gossip has already injured and wounded my spirit and I cannot ignore it, I usually find peace after simply talking it over with my Lord. I do not concern myself even over what may be serious sin unless I know 100 percent for sure that what I have heard is true and God has definitely shown me that it is my responsibility to take it to an authority. Usually, God does not give us a responsibility for disciplining sin unless He has also given us authority.

For example, because I am a mother and have a position of authority over my children, I am given by God the responsibility to correct their weaknesses and sins from time to time. God has not, however, given me authority over other's children. Because of this, I very rarely correct a child who is not my own. I would, however, correct a student who is in my Sunday school class because, again, God has given me the authority to do so. I would not correct him in the same way that I would my own child because I do not have as much authority over him. Some people make many enemies because of considering it their responsibility to correct another's child.

I do not meddle in every bit of strife that takes place between my own children and their friends. Anyone who works with children, especially very small children, knows that there are squabbles among them. Yes, we should teach our children to get along with others, but if we meddle in all of their strifes, we will lose our sanity and will not be able to work with groups of children effectively.

I try not to meddle in the occasional strife that my husband must encounter in his work. I try simply to brag on him and to encourage him in his ability to get along with others.

(7) **When you must respond to sin, respond with a well thought-out and prepared statement.** Jesus thought long and hard before He responded to the accusations against the adulterous woman. He then made just one brief statement.

If we need to rebuke someone for his sin, we should plan our correction and make it as brief as possible. This is why I do not believe in grounding a child for six months or even six weeks. A child makes a mistake and is still being punished for it six months later. The punishment should be brief.

A wife and mother who cares will plan to brag on her loved ones as she corrects their problems. She will plan to relate with the interests of her loved one. She will plan to make statements that express her feelings and that do not sound like accusations. (For example, try replacing the word "you" in the statement with the words "I feel.") She will delete unkind words from her statement. She might even use an illustration or a visual aid to explain the problem. She will even prepare herself for a negative reaction from her loved one and will plan how to keep her temper under control.

(8) **Complete your confrontation with sin by again identifying with the sinner.** Jesus made his well-thought and brief statement, and He again stooped down to the ground. It is always a good idea to confront a small child's sin by getting down to their eye level. And it is a good idea to end a negative conversation by again expressing your own mistakes and failures, perhaps even in the area of a similar problem.

Allow me to share with you a verse in Proverbs which the Lord showed me when I was struggling in knowing how to respond to a sin of another. Proverbs 14:16 says, *"A wise man feareth, and departeth from evil: but the fool rageth, and is confident."*

A wise man or woman realizes when she hears of a sin committed that she herself could have committed that sin. She reacts to the sins of others by planning some precautions which would prevent her from making the same mistake.

A fool becomes angry and disgusted when he hears about the sins of others, and he is confident that he would never do the same thing. Sounds like the scribes and Pharisees in this story, doesn't it?! As we see in this story, usually those who bark loudest about the sins of others are the most guilty themselves.

(9) **Remember that proper handling of sin is convicting.** Self-righteous anger usually leads the person deeper into their sin. It causes children to go further astray from their parents, and it destroys marriages.

When Jesus dealt with sin, every person became convicted by his own sin. The adulterous woman felt very loved by Jesus, and yet, I believe, she obeyed Jesus' admonition to *"...go, and sin no more."*

(10) **Handle the sins of others by forgiving and restoring the sinner.** Jesus forgave and then restored the adulterous woman. Our goal in handling sin, when it is our responsibility to do so, should be to restore the sinner to complete fellowship and to forgive him.

REACTING PROPERLY TO SIN

A parent who does not express affection, love and forgiveness after punishing his child has not punished properly. I expect my children to spontaneously weep and hug me after I have punished them. If they do not, I believe that I have failed to punish them properly, and something must be well-thought-out and changed.

The Devil often uses a good thing to destroy good people or to make them less effective for Christ. If the Devil destroys me, it probably will not be through drugs or alcohol. It could be, but it probably will not be. Why? Because I have never tried either, and at this stage of my Christian life, it would be difficult to be tempted in this area. I remind you it would not be impossible, but it would not be the easiest way.

The Devil would more likely try to destroy me by allowing me to become self-righteous and bitter about the actual sins which I know others to have committed. Therefore, I must not allow the accusations which I hear to "shake me up." Rather, I must at all times stay close in fellowship to my Lord and seek to handle accusations as He would have me to.

I have a responsibility to be a help to my husband and a nurturer and trainer to my children. I will lose them, though, if I cannot do this humbly. What a responsibility for one who is a sinner herself to show her children the right and godly way. I pray that I would do so as Jesus did in John 8—I pray I would do it with humility and with grace. Let us correct as few sins as we can. When we must correct, let us do so while preserving the dignity and the self-respect of those we love.

Avenge Me of My Adversary

A Lesson From
the Avenged Widow

"And shall not God avenge his own elect,
which cry day and night unto him,
though he bear long with them?"
(Luke 18:7)

Chapter 17
The Avenged Widow
Luke 18:1-8

ECAUSE I HAVE been a preacher's daughter for all of my 36 years and my preacher father has been in the limelight of old-fashioned fundamentalism, I know what it is like to have adversaries. Though my family has been blessed by God with many special and faithful friends in our stand for Christ, there have also been those people who have been actively hostile to us.

Perhaps that is why I find the story of the avenged widow in Luke chapter 18 so interesting and important. You see, there have been times when I, too, have come to my Judge wanting to know just what to do with my adversaries. I'm sure you can identify. What person is there on this earth who has not known, at some time, the active hostility of another person? What person has not wondered just what to do in response to an attack?

When I finished studying the widow in Luke 18, I was both thrilled and blessed to discover that God had some clear information on how to handle adversaries. In my late twenties and early thirties, my husband and I endured some especially difficult times with my parents in their ministry. I have wondered many times if I was handling my parents' trials and their adversaries correctly. In Luke 18, I found answers to my questions which I believe can be helpful to us all. Please allow me to share with you what the Bible says about handling your adversaries.

1   **When you are being attacked by an adversary, stay in an attitude of prayer at all times.** Jesus used the story of the avenged widow and the judge to teach us *"...that men ought always to pray, and not to faint."* (Luke 18:1b) I used to read this verse and wonder how it was possible to pray all of the time. In the last few years, however, I have learned to stay in an attitude of prayer all the time.

I get up between 5:00 and 5:30 every morning and start my prayer time with God. I have a time when I pray alone on my knees early each morning. During this time, I do nothing but pray. However, I also pray each morning as I fix my hair, get dressed, and put on my makeup. I pray as I drive home from taking my children to school each morning and as I go to pick them up each afternoon.

I have several times during the day when I ask Jesus to forgive me of my sins and when I yield again to the Holy Spirit. I also listen to at least one sermon each day I am at home. I make sure that everything I see or hear throughout my day puts me in an attitude of prayer rather than stealing my heart away from the Lord.

You may say, "My, you must be a wonderful Christian!" No, I do not necessarily do these things because I am a good Christian; I do these things because I need to pray always in order to survive as a Christian. You see, I have adversaries. When I get up and have my quiet time with the Lord each morning, my faith in God and my love toward my adversaries is strong. Have you ever noticed, though, how the love we feel in our hearts in our early morning devotions often wanes by 3:00 or so in the afternoon? Why is that? It's because we are too weak as Christians to love our adversaries by taking just one "shot" of prayer a day. We need our Physician to "inject" us several times. Especially is this true when we are enduring an openly hostile attack from someone who considers himself to be our enemy.

I must admit that I have not attained in this area, but I believe that a person who needs to be avenged of an adversary must stay in an attitude of prayer all day long. Staying in an attitude of prayer prevents me from thinking badly or talking badly about my adversaries. It also keeps my heart loving toward them.

2 **Do not allow yourself to become weary of Satan's attacks.** Luke 18:1 says that men ought *"...not to faint."* My dictionary tells me that the word *faint* means "to lose courage or hope; to lose purpose or enthusiasm; to lose brightness." The Bible is teaching us that the only way we can keep from losing our brightness and our enthusiasm during times of attack is to stay in a continual attitude of prayer.

I admire my dad tremendously for the fact that he has not lost his brightness even though he has been subject to countless attacks in his ministry. You don't have to look very closely to see a twinkle in Dad's eye. You will not have to listen to him long before you hear his rousing laughter and learn that he has a wonderful sense of humor. What is it that has allowed my dad to keep his brightness when under attack? The answer is PRAYER!

If you ever heard my dad preach, you no doubt noticed that he never lost his bold style of "telling it like is it." You also noticed that his purpose did not diminish because of increased attack; rather, it was enhanced. No matter what the Devil hurls my way, I want to radiate a brightness for Christ. I want to serve with purpose, courage, and enthusiasm. I do not wish to allow an adversary to cause me to faint. What is it that will keep me from fainting? It's prayer!

3 **Realize that when God does avenge you, it will often be brought about by someone whom you least expect God to use.** The widow was avenged by an unjust judge. The Bible does not tell us that the judge avenged the widow because he had recently gotten saved and was feeling convicted. No, the Bible tells us that the judge avenged the widow even though he didn't fear God.

When we are attacked by an enemy, we do not need to go around looking for someone to avenge us. God will not avenge us until He is ready. When He does avenge us, He can use even a heathen like the unjust judge to do it.

One of my favorite stories in the Bible is the story of Moses' delivering the children of Israel from wicked Pharaoh. Have you ever thought about whom God used to "put Moses' foot in the door"? God used Pharaoh's own daughter to rear the man who would deliver the children of Israel from Pharaoh. Truly God must have laughed in Heaven over that one. We don't need to frantically look for deliverance when we are under attack. We only need to anticipate the surprise of whom God will use to deliver us.

(4) Do not seek to clear your reputation or to make others respect you. I realize there is a time to reply to the attacks of an adversary, but the judge who avenged the widow in Luke 18 did not do so because he had come to respect the widow. The Bible tells us that the unjust judge did not regard man. If we go around trying to find someone who will listen to our side of the story, we will surely lose our brightness and our purpose. We need to trust God to avenge us, knowing that He can clear our reputation if and when He chooses. Our responsibility is to serve Him and to stay close to Him. The amazing thing is that God can use someone who does not even particularly like us to avenge us of our adversary. What an exciting and surprising God we have!

(5) Trouble God with your hurt. The Bible tells us that the unjust judge avenged the widow only because he was tired of her troubling him. I am so glad God used the word "trouble" there. My Bible dictionary tells me that the verb *trouble* means *to disturb, pester* and *stir up*.

Have you ever spent so much time with someone or asked someone for something so many times that you were sure you were pestering him? Yet in Luke 18, God is trying to teach us to pester Him. He wants to be pestered by me! As a mother, I can understand this a little. I allow my children to pester me and even enjoy it most of the time. I must admit that there have been times when I gave them something that I knew was not best for them because I was "pestered" into doing it. However, even I as a mother grow weary of the disturbances of my own offspring. Yet here is the Almighty God trying to teach me in His Word to pester Him and promising me that if I will disturb Him enough, He will avenge me of my adversaries.

I have been told a few times in my life that something about which I was praying was a matter about which I should not bother God. When I studied the avenged widow, I was thrilled to realize that God wants to be troubled. I try to make it clear to my Lord that I do not wish Him to ever answer a prayer that would not be His will for me. Yet I find great delight in knowing that I can *pester, disturb* and *stir up* my God about anything. Also, I find that pestering God with my troubles keeps me from taking troubles to my husband, children and loved ones, which would discourage them. It works best when I take my troubles to the One Who can always do something about them.

6 **Schedule one time in the day and one time in the evening to ask God to avenge you of your adversary.** Luke 18:7 says that God avenges those who *"...cry day and night unto him...."* Perhaps I am taking this verse too literally, but following this interpretation is certainly not a bad idea. At least two times during each 24-hour period, I ask God to avenge me of my loved ones' adversaries. I am not talking here about asking God to punish someone who just hurt my own personal feelings. I am talking about asking God to protect us and to avenge us, if necessary, of those who have launched an attack on my church and on those I love.

I call before the Lord the names of those who are actively hostile toward us. I do not call their names in front of my loved ones. The names of these adversaries would be unfamiliar to my children. Nor do I take other time to think about adversaries. If I saw them on the street, I would greet them with a friendly hello and a smile. I would not take time to chat or socialize, but I would not be unkind.

7 **Seek out the whole Truth of God.** My adversaries have done me a favor in that they have turned me toward the Bible. My relationship with the Bible has never been sweeter, and this is important because Luke 18:8 tells us that as the coming of Christ draws nearer, few will be the people who have faith. The word *faith* here is talking about "complete belief in the whole Truth of God." It is our faith and knowledge of God's Word that will give us patience as we wait to be avenged of our adversaries.

8 **Realize that God bears long with those who are being attacked.** This may not sound like good news to those who understand the word *bear* to mean "refraining from power." But the word *bear* has another meaning. It also means "to support." God may be a while in avenging us, but He will also be supporting us all the while. He will give us the strength we need to wait to be avenged.

9 **Realize that God will avenge us speedily.** The word *speedily* speaks of "ratio of performance"—meaning that when God does avenge us, the swiftness of His vengeance will make the length of time we spent waiting seem to be very short. Let me give you an example:

When I was a young girl, I began to ask God for something very important, but He chose not to answer my prayer. He chose not to give me the thing for which I was asking. I asked God for this particular prayer to be answered almost every day of my life for 22 years. After 22 years, God answered my prayer both swiftly and completely. If you were to ask me if I minded the wait, I would answer with the question, "What wait?" You see, the time I spent praying for an answer seems very short now when compared to the swiftness and the sweetness with which God answered my prayer. So it will seem to us when God finally avenges us of our adversaries.

10 **Realize that we all really have only one adversary—Satan.** Someday God will speedily avenge us of our only enemy—the Devil. He is our only real enemy, and we must not confuse him with those well-meaning friends who hurt our feelings and attack our reputations.

I must admit that there have been times when I have allowed the Devil to use me to hurt one of God's people. Most, if not all of those times, it has been unintentional on my part. I hope those whom I have hurt will realize that I am not the Devil incarnate. I hope they can find forgiveness and patience in their hearts for me.

So it is with many people who have acted as my adversaries. Many of them were simply friends whom the Devil used to attack me or maybe just to neglect me or forget me. I must remember at these times that it is the Devil who is my adversary, not my friends. I do believe that some of my parents' adversaries have been heathen and ungodly people. Yet whoever the adversary, it is Satan who is behind the destruction of our reputations and the hurt feelings. Because of this, every day I ask God to teach me to hate Satan more; and I ask God to avenge me of my adversary, the Devil.

God promises that He will avenge us speedily. This means that someday I will probably ask my parents in Heaven something like this: "Do you remember all the trouble that Satan caused you when we were on earth?" I will not be surprised if they answer, "Satan? Who's that?"

Though we wait long for God to avenge us of our adversary, someday God will avenge us so swiftly that we will hardly remember the trouble our adversary caused us. Until that wonderful time when we will be avenged of all our adversaries, let's handle Satan's attacks and each enemy like the Lord would have us to handle them.

Why We Do
What We Do

A Lesson From Sapphira

"*For the* LORD *seeth not as man seeth;*
for man looketh on the outward appearance,
but the LORD *looketh on the heart.*"
(I Samuel 16:7b)

Chapter 18
Sapphira
Acts 5:1 - 11

SAPPHIRA AND HER husband Ananias had a secret. They had sold some land and had promised the Holy Spirit that they would give all of the profit from the sale of the land to God. Both husband and wife knew when Ananias presented the profit to the apostles that he had only given part of it. But Ananias made it appear as though they had given all.

The Holy Spirit revealed to Peter what had happened, and Peter asked Ananias why he had lied to the Spirit. "...*Why hast thou conceived this thing in thine heart? thou hast not lied unto men, but unto God.*"

As soon as Ananias heard Peter's words, he fell down dead. Three hours later, after Ananias had already been carried out and buried, Sapphira appeared. Peter asked her whether she had sold the land for a certain price.

Sapphira lied and said, "Yes." She wanted to make it look as though she and her husband had given it all, when actually the land had been sold for more.

Peter asked, "*How is it that ye have agreed together to tempt the Spirit of the Lord?*" He predicted Sapphira's death, and she died instantly. She, too, was immediately carried out and buried. And the Bible says, "*And great fear came upon all the church, and upon as many as heard these things.*"

In this account, we have a lesson on two important terms: vows and motives.

Why We Do What We Do

Vows

"It is a snare to the man who devoureth that which is holy, and after vows to make enquiry." (Proverbs 20:25)

A man (or a woman) becomes ensnared in sin when he takes that which is holy or that which is promised to God and uses it for himself. Sometimes a person begins to hold back what he has promised to God, or he begins to question whether or not his vow was really what the Lord wanted. When this begins to happen, the wise person will realize that these questions are really a snare or a trap from the Devil. Once something is promised to God, it is His; it cannot be taken back.

We should never undo in doubt the promises we have made to God in faith. Not only should we not do it, but we **cannot** do it. Once something belongs to God, it is His. What causes us to hold back from God what we have promised to Him?

(1) **Selfishness or greed causes us to hold back from God what we have promised to Him.** I have promised my life to the Lord. Because of that, I realize that no decision I make in my life can be based on material gain. My decisions must be based on what God wants.

I have two children whom I gave to God at their births. At this writing, my oldest is now 15, and I can see that it can be tempting to hold my children back from doing God's will. It would be so pleasant to have my children and future grandchildren living nearby. They could serve God, but couldn't it be in the same ministry where we serve rather than on some foreign mission field?

It, of course, would not be wrong for them to serve close to where their dad and I serve. That is often God's will for families, and I am happy for them. I would definitely be very happy to have my children near me. Yet, I do not want to encourage my children to hold back from doing exactly what God wants them to do.

Our selfishness often manifests in the way of materialism as it did in Sapphira's life. God has put my husband and me in a lovely home, but home, money and possessions have never been that upon which we have built our choices.

I dream of my daughter being able to be a wonderful homemaker in a lovely home. Still, God may call her far away where her home would be one with a thatched roof, rather than a home which would fulfill my American dream for her. Even though I may be tempted, I will not encourage my children to hold back from God regarding material things. I must be a good example in this area by holding loosely to my home and possessions. I must put the priority of caring for these things in God's order and not in my own.

(2) **Lack of faith often causes us to hold back from God what we have promised to Him.** Questions sometimes come to my mind such as, "What if God calls my children to a land where the life expectancy is short?" (For instance, the island of Haiti, where my daughter has expressed interest in going as a missionary, has an average life expectancy of 35.) What if my child becomes very ill and dies? What if my grandchildren have health problems? What if their lives are endangered?

Faith ignores and refuses to receive the questions which the Devil puts in our mind. We must remember that these questions are the Devil's traps. Faith remembers, instead, the promises God has made to us and the promises we have made to Him.

Motives

"...For the LORD seeth not as man seeth; for man looketh on the outward appearance, but the LORD looketh on the heart."
(I Samuel 16:7b)

Ananias and Sapphira's primary concern wasn't whether or not they had kept their promise to God. Their concern was not in giving to God. Their concern was in what people thought. As long as Peter and the other apostles thought that they had given all, nothing else mattered.

Many wives and mothers only give to God to the degree that it will make them appear righteous before other men and women. Of course, we would not want our children to use drugs or drink liquor. How would that look to our fellow church members? They might not think we were good parents.

As long as our children are good, upstanding citizens, it appears that we have done a good job of parenting. Only God knows if we have held them back by discouraging them from doing greater things for Him.

As long as my husband is a good, decent family man, it appears that I am a good wife before others. Only God knows whether I have discouraged him from being a fanatic. (After all, what would the neighbors think?)

None of us has pure motives before God. Though I so often pray and ask God to give me proper motives, especially as I care for my family, I **do** care what people think of me as a wife and a mother. I do not spend a lot of time analyzing my motives. Nor do I think that those of us who have impure motives will be bereft of rewards when we meet Christ.

I do believe, however, that those of us who are not growing in our love for Christ will be more tempted to hold back from God. Why? Because love for Christ is the only motive which will keep us going for God every time we are tempted to hold back from Him. *"Blessed is the man that endureth temptation: for when he is tried, he shall receive the crown of life, which the Lord hath promised to them that love him."* (James 1:12)

There was a season in my life when I was especially tempted to hold back from God. During that season, I slept at night with my head on my Bible where it was opened to James 1:12.

Since I was eight years old, I have been growing in my walk with God and in my love for God. Though my motives are often filled more with pride than with love, I know it is my love relationship with God which has prevented me from holding back my life and my family from Him.

Let me also add that God holds me responsible not only when I hold back from Him, but also when I am privy to my husband's holding back. I cannot lead or control my husband, but God will hold me responsible for encouraging him to hold back or for discouraging him from giving all. It was Ananias, the husband, who actually gave only part of the money to Peter. But both were privy to it, and both were killed.

Lastly, I want to say that the result of Ananias' and Sapphira's punishment and death was fear by all. God punishes sin because He wants others to hear and to fear. God does not want us to respond to other's sin and punishment with a self-confident or with a critical attitude. He wants *all* of us to fear when we hear of His judgment.

We are all plagued with impure motives. Let us continually seek to know Christ and to love Him more so that we might not hold back from all the blessing and service He has planned for us and for our families.

I Want to Be Missed

A Lesson From Dorcas

"Yea, saith the Spirit,
that they may rest from their labours;
and their works do follow them."
(Revelation 14:13b)

Chapter 19

Dorcas

Acts 9:36 - 43

WHEN I DIE, I want my husband to miss me. People often say that it is a compliment to a deceased wife when her husband marries again quickly. I am not sure that I want my husband to compliment me that much. I have even heard of a wife's choosing a wife for her husband before she passed away. I am not sure I could do that.

Dorcas (or Tabitha) is a good example of a woman who was missed when she died. Dorcas was a woman whom the Bible says "...*was full of good works....*" She became sick and died and was laid in an upper chamber. The disciples sent for Peter who was in a town nearby. When Peter came to Dorcas, he found all the widows near her crying over her death. The widows showed Peter the coats and the other garments that Dorcas had made them.

Peter sent the women away, and then he knelt down beside Dorcas and began to pray. He turned to Dorcas' body and said, "...*Tabitha, arise....*" Dorcas opened her eyes and she sat up. Peter gave her his hand, and he lifted her up. Then he called in the saints and presented her alive. Many people were saved as a result of Dorcas' resurrection from the dead.

Allow me to share with you some lessons from Dorcas' life about how to be missed.

 A woman who is full of good works is more likely to be missed by others. Some people are missed when they are gone because they are famous and have done some well-known deed in their lives. But this cannot be the case with everyone. Some people get so busy trying to do some great deed that they never accomplish much for God at all. In the process, they may step on other people in order to achieve their goal. This type of person does not build enough close relationships to be missed by others.

The Christian life is not to be lived so that greatness and fame can be reached. Rather, a Christian is supposed to be full of good works each day. Each day a Christian must spend his time doing every moment the good things that God would have him to do. Each day a Christian should be seeking to bestow good works upon others.

A Christian should not seek to be great, but he should seek to be good. Greatness, I believe, is stumbled upon on the path of goodness.

Proverbs 16:9 says, *"A man's heart deviseth his way: but the LORD directeth his steps."* Man often dreams of greatness, even regarding his spiritual life. God doesn't mind our dreaming of doing great things for Him. But most of all, He wants us to follow Him one step at a time. He wants us to be satisfied to do His will in small ways by doing good one day at a time.

2 **A woman who gives is more likely to be missed by others.** Dorcas gave beautiful garments to others. It was these beautiful garments that the saints showed to Peter as they wept over Dorcas' death. When people envision greatness, they rarely envision giving, but I guarantee you that God does. Most people's idea of personal success is wrapped up in visions of personal gain or of some great personal accomplishment. Often God sees the successful Christian as one who gives away (or loses) or as one who gives up his own success in order to see the success of others.

This pretty well describes the role of a wife and a mother. She gives and she gives and then she gives some more. She goes without pretty clothes or buys less expensive ones so that her children can dress nicely.

She runs up and down the stairs and in and out of the rooms of her house so that she can wait upon her family. Most of this service is done toward the end of the day when she is already worn to a frazzle.

She makes her choices in life with this thought in mind: "Will this bring me success at the expense of the success of my husband or children?" If the answer is "yes," then she says "no" to her own opportunities.

Does a woman have to live this way? No, she does not; and I must admit that I often grow weary of giving and giving and giving to those I love. It is then that I remember the following verses:

> *"Let nothing be done through strife or vainglory; but in lowliness of mind let each esteem other better than themselves.*
>
> *Look not every man on his own things, but every man also on the things of others.*
>
> *Let this mind be in you, which was also in Christ Jesus:*
>
> *Who, being in the form of God, thought it not robbery to be equal with God:*
>
> *But made himself of no reputation, and took upon him the form of a servant, and was made in the likeness of men."*
>
> *And being found in fashion as a man, he humbled himself, and became obedient unto death, even the death of the cross."*
>
> (Philippians 2:3-8)

Philippians 2:9 tells us that **because** of Jesus' servanthood, God has highly exalted Him. *"Wherefore God also hath highly exalted him, and given him a name which is above every name."*

Giving to my family gives me the opportunity to be like Jesus. And it also gives me greater opportunity to receive God's blessing upon my life. Matthew 20:27 says, *"And whosoever will be chief among you, let him be your servant."*

The definition of the word *servant* in my dictionary simply says "to subject." The Bible commands wives to be in subjection to their own husbands in Ephesians 5:22. God is commanding us to be our husband's servant. Because the wife and mother has been given the servant role in the home, she has the most opportunity to become great. Greatness is in serving.

I Want to Be Missed

I ask God to crucify my flesh each day and to help me to die to self so that I might unselfishly serve my family. Why? Not only because I want to attain true Bible greatness, but also because I want to be the kind of wife and mother whose presence is missed.

3 **A woman who uses her talents for others is more likely to be missed.** Dorcas' talent was in being a seamstress. She did not use this talent just for herself, but she also used it for many others. The modern woman uses her talents to get ahead in the world. The Christian woman should use her talents for others more than she uses them for herself. People have a tendency to need and to miss this type of lady. We also need to remember that even if we do not have a lot of talent or a lot of money, we can still **do** good works.

4 **A woman who gives to the poor and to the needy is more likely to be missed than others.** It was not a huge crowd who gathered around Dorcas' dead body. It was not a rich crowd who gathered around her. It was just a crowd of poor widows. But if Dorcas had not cared for those widows, she would not have been raised from the dead. It was the mourning of the widows which caused others to go and seek Peter.

Many people want to get ahead by seeking out great crowds. They seek the well-known or the influential people as friends in order to achieve greatness. Now there is certainly nothing wrong with being kind to those who are great and well-known. But Jesus spent most of His earthly life with the poor. He was even born into a poor family.

Women often do not wish to stay at home and train their children because they are just children. As they minister to their small brood of little ones, mothers often feel that God has put them on a shelf. Perhaps God does not consider them worthy to be used in as great a way as some other woman. But greatness comes from doing good to the small crowds and to the people who need us the most, though they may have the least to offer us.

Let me close by saying this: God did use Dorcas to do something great eventually. Dorcas' resurrection from the dead was heard all throughout the land, and many people were saved. Not only did Dorcas do something great, but she also became famous. (Her story, after all, is in the Bible.) But it was the many, many things which Dorcas did that were **good** which made her great. If she had not been full of good works bestowed upon a small group of poor widows, she could never have been great.

Let us as wives and mothers not seek greatness for ourselves. Rather, let us fill each of our days with good works done for those who need us most. In doing so, will we perhaps achieve greatness? Yes, we definitely will; for in doing so, we will become more like the Saviour Himself.

...And in doing so, we will develop close and personal relationships which will make such an impact that we will be missed by others. It's a good thing, because I really, really want to be missed.

Don't Forget to Believe

A Lesson From Rhoda

"And when she knew Peter's voice,
she opened not the gate for gladness,
but ran in, and told how Peter stood before the gate."
(Acts 12:14)

Chapter 20
Rhoda
Acts 12:12 - 17

THE STORY OF Rhoda in the Bible is a wonderful story of how God can use an absent-minded young girl. I am surely glad that He can. As I have already admitted in a previous chapter, I am one of those absent-minded ones. I have a trait which I believe is usually a masculine one. I have an extremely one-track mind. I find it difficult to think of more than one thing at a time.

I learned to do only one thing at a time when my now 15-year-old daughter Jaclynn was only a baby. It was a Wednesday afternoon, and I was going to fry chicken for the evening meal. I put some cooking oil on the stove in a frying pan and left it to heat up a bit. I decided to dress my baby daughter for the Wednesday evening church service while the oil was heating. I accidentally forgot the oil, and by the time I remembered it, I found flames rising in my kitchen. I **did** have the presence of mind to put out the flames with some baking soda. But because the house was already filled with thick smoke, I had to call the fire department. They arrived with three trucks just before my husband arrived home from work. You can imagine his surprise and concern when he saw three fire engines in our driveway. (That's what you get for marrying an absent-minded woman—an interesting life!)

Last April I left my sunglasses at my mom and dad's house. I had to stop by their house early on a Sunday morning to deliver a cake, and though I was only in their house for a few seconds, I managed to set down my glasses and leave them. My family and I returned to my mom and dad's house on Sunday afternoon to eat lunch together and to celebrate my daughter's birthday. I retrieved my sunglasses when I arrived, but by the time I left to go home, I had forgotten my sunglasses, and I left them at my parents' house again.

I stopped by my dad's office at church after the Sunday evening service and found my sunglasses in his office refrigerator. You see, my mother had given him instructions to return them to me. He was afraid that he would forget to give them to me. Because he always gets me something to drink when I come to his office, he put my sunglasses in the refrigerator where he would not forget them. I guess my dad can be a little absent-minded also!

Rhoda had a similar problem. I believe it is a problem for which Rhoda is still "teased"—even though several centuries after her life have passed!

Here is her story: The church was gathered at the home of Mary, the mother of John Mark. Their purpose for being there was to pray that Peter would be delivered from jail. God answered their prayers and miraculously delivered him. The first place Peter headed was to Mary's house. Perhaps he knew the people would be praying for him there.

Peter knocked on the door, and it was the little girl Rhoda who heard his knock. Though there were many people gathered in the house, Rhoda answered the door. Rhoda recognized Peter's voice, and instead of answering the door and greeting Peter, she ran to tell the others in the house that he was at the door.

The others did not believe that it was Peter. They told Rhoda that it was Peter's angel. They supposed that Peter had been killed. As Rhoda tried to convince the church people that it was indeed Peter at the door, the people told her she was crazy. Yet the Bible says that Rhoda "...constantly affirmed that it was even so."

As Peter continued knocking, the folks finally opened the door and saw that, yes, it was Peter. There is a lot of humanity in this story. It is so human for a group of people to gather for the sole purpose of praying for a miracle to take place and then to be quite shocked that the miracle actually did take place. So many times I have been shocked when God answered even the smallest of my prayers. It is as if I don't believe that the Creator of all the universe can take care of my trivial problems.

There is also a lot of humor in this story. The Bible even seems to point out the joke when it says in Acts 12:14, *"And when she knew Peter's voice, she opened not the gate for gladness, but ran in, and told how Peter stood before the gate."*

I'm sure Peter was anxious to have a hiding place, and I'm sure he was anxious to see folks that loved him and to share with them what God had just done in his life. But instead, he stood knocking and knocking and knocking while a group of people argued about whether it really could be he. They argued about whether or not God really could answer their prayers.

There is a bit of humor in Rhoda's life. Her absent-minded life, like mine, surely was interesting—very interesting. But her life is also full of good lessons which can be learned from what Rhoda did **not** forget. Allow me to share them with you.

1 **Rhoda did not forget to listen at the door.** The Bible tells us in Acts 12:12 that *"...many were gathered together praying."* But there was only one young girl who *"...came to hearken...."* (verse 13) I not only want to pray and to believe, but I want to be expecting, to be watching, and to be listening for an answer to my prayer.

2 **Rhoda did not forget to answer the door.** Again, Rhoda was the only one who answered the door.

My dad often advises people who have been praying for a baby for many years to demonstrate their faith in God by actually acting upon their prayers. He encourages them to prepare a nursery as if they were already expecting a child. I know of some couples who have done this and whom God has blessed with a baby shortly thereafter.

Of course, we must accept God's will for our lives, and sometimes, it does not include that for which we ask. But we should be looking for the answer to our prayers.

My husband preaches that God answers every prayer that we pray, and I believe this to be true. Many times we don't realize that He answered because we were not looking for His answer. Or perhaps we were only looking for the answer as we would have it.

My husband uses this illustration: a man may pray for a new car. God may answer his prayer by causing his old car to have a flat tire. God is, perhaps, trying to show this man that His will is not to give a new car to the man at this time, but instead to make the man more Christ-like by giving Him trouble with his old car.

I believe this man should continue praying for the new car. He should also be accepting of whatever God's will may be for his life. And he should be listening for God's answer in whatever way that it will come. The man or woman who is listening for all of God's answers can better communicate with God and know God's workings in his life.

3 **Rhoda did not forget to recognize Peter's voice.** Rhoda knew the preacher's voice. She obviously was well acquainted with the preacher.

I want my children to know the men of God very well. I am fortunate to have a wonderful preacher who is my husband and the father of my children. My children are very close to their dad. They have been taught to honor him and to honor their grandfather, who is also a preacher. They have been encouraged to make heroes of preachers and to seek the advice of God's men, even those other than their father and grandfather. I believe that knowing men of God can definitely strengthen one's faith.

4 **Rhoda did not forget to believe Peter was at the door.** She did not forget to tell the others that it was Peter. Rhoda, in her simple child-like faith, was quick to believe that Peter was indeed at the door. I pray often for God to strengthen my faith and to give me a simple child-like faith. A child is so quick to believe that if God says it can happen, it can really happen.

(5) **Rhoda did not forget to confirm her faith to others.** The people told Rhoda she was crazy, but she continued to express her faith in God and to try to confirm the others' faith.

The others were not convinced that God could answer their prayers, but Rhoda continued to try to convince them that God had answered their prayers and that God did work miracles.

In this instance, Rhoda **may** have had even more faith than Peter himself. The Bible tells us that Peter thought he was only dreaming when he first was delivered from prison. An angel smote him, but he did not believe. The chains miraculously fell off his hands, but he did not believe. An angel led him past the first gate, past the second get and to an iron gate. The gates opened to him "...*of his own accord.*" Still Peter did not believe. Peter passed through one street, and then the Bible tells us that Peter finally came to himself. In this instance Rhoda's spirit may have been even more optimistic and full of faith than was Peter's.

I pray that I would not be a pessimist, but rather an optimist like Rhoda was. I believe that pessimism is the number one reason why people fall into depression. They think not only that things are bad, but also that they are going to get worse. They may pray, but they have forgotten to believe. Pessimistic people have no hope.

Instead, I want to believe that things will go well and that God does answer every prayer we pray for our best, even if it hurts sometimes. People may think I'm dead wrong; they may even think I'm crazy, but I want to continue to confirm my own faith and the faith of others.

So you see, Rhoda's life was not such a foolish one after all. Sure she may have forgotten to let Peter in the door right away. But she remembered the most important thing for salvation and the most important thing for life: she remembered to believe.

Ephesians 2:8, 9, "*For by grace are ye saved through faith; and that not of yourselves: it is the gift of God: Not of works, lest any man should boast.*"

John 3:16, *"For God so loved the world, that he gave his only begotten Son, that whosoever believeth in him should not perish, but have everlasting life."*

Hebrews 11:6, *"But without faith it is impossible to please him: for he that cometh to God must believe that he is, and that he is a rewarder of them that diligently seek him."*

Remember to Believe

But to be honest, there are many areas in my life where I, as a wife and a mother, find it difficult to remember to believe. They are as follows:

A. *I forget to believe God can bless and protect my marriage.* In this generation, there have been so many marriage failures, even among Christians, that sometimes I forget to believe in what God can do in my own marriage. Even preachers' marriages have failed, which should come as no surprise. We are all just flesh.

I have even been warned by well-meaning preachers to guard the purity of myself and of my husband. Though I pray daily that God would protect both my husband's purity and my purity and that He would bless our marriage, sometimes I forget to believe.

I find it easier to remember the marriages which **have** failed than I do to remember to believe that mine can succeed. I often have to remind myself to let go of my worries and fears and to remember not only to pray for a good marriage, but also to believe for one.

B. *I forget to believe that my children can turn out right.* Psalm 127:1 and 2 say, *"Except the LORD build the house, they labour in vain that build it: except the LORD keep the city, the watchman waketh but in vain. It is vain for you to rise up early, to sit up late, to eat the bread of sorrows: for so he giveth his beloved sleep."*

God does not wish us to "worry" our children for the Lord; He wishes us to rear them for the Lord. In our generation, so many children have disappointed their parents that it is easier to remember to worry than it is to remember to believe. I pray for my children to do God's will. I pray that this will be for God's glory and not for mine. I pray God will give my husband and me power to rear our children properly. I also tell God that I believe He will answer my prayer. *I am trying to remember to believe!*

C. *I forget to believe that God can use me as well as my family.* I can remember one wife's telling me that she did not believe her husband would make a good pastor or assistant pastor. I'm sure she was quite shocked when her husband became an assistant pastor of a large church. I wonder sometimes how much more God could use our husbands if we forgot about their bad breath in the morning, their smelly feet at night; and remembered instead to believe in them and, even more so, to believe in the God of our prayers.

I wonder what God could do with our children if we reared them not only with prayer, but also with a vision. We need to rear them with a vision not of who they are or of who their parents are. We need to rear them with a vision of what God can do—the God Who answers all of our prayers. He is the God Who wants to work good in our lives and the God Who wants to bless.

I wonder what God could do with the wives and mothers who read this book if they quit wallowing in the mire of low self-esteem. If they would forget to remember their many weaknesses for a while and glory instead in the strength of their God, the possibilities would indeed be endless.

Rhoda, Rhoda, Rhoda...how absent-minded you are! You forgot...but you forgot for a very good reason. You forgot to let Peter in because you were excited about your faith. You were excited to tell others about God's answer to prayer.

I am sure to forget many, many more things in my life, and it is sure to be very interesting. After all, I haven't even reached old age yet! But should I forget everything else, I pray that I will remember the most important thing. I pray that, like Rhoda, I will never forget to believe.

Constraining Power

A Lesson From Lydia

"For the love of Christ constraineth us."
(II Corinthians 5:14a)

Chapter 21
Lydia
Acts 16:14, 15

LYDIA WAS A seller of purple, a fine silk-like fabric, which the Lord describes as a fabric befitting a real lady. This leads me to imagine that Lydia was a real lady—a classy kind of a lady. Although Lydia was not saved, she had the character to work hard and the religious desire to worship God. This also leads me to believe that she was indeed a classy lady.

God blessed Lydia's actions which were based upon the knowledge she already had, and He opened her heart to pay attention to the words of Paul. She was saved and immediately baptized and so was her entire family. What an influence Lydia must have had on her family.

After Lydia was saved and baptized, the Bible says that she sought for Paul and for those who were with him and she constrained them to abide in her house. Lydia was hospitable—another quality of a lady with class. But the most classy trait Lydia had—the thing which attracts my attention the most—is the way she constrained others. ("...*And she constrained us.*" [Acts 16:15]) My dictionary defines the word *constrain* like this: "to urge with irresistible power." What wife or mother would not like to have this kind of constraining power over her family?

Husbands, who are made in the image of Jesus, need to be constrained. The male ego is such that it rarely displays its power before being convinced that power is needed. When a wife fails to constrain her husband or fails to make him feel that he is needed, it becomes difficult to motivate him to perform for her and to be the strength that she needs.

Jesus needed to be constrained. In Luke 24:28-30, the Bible says that Jesus pretended that He was going to leave the disciples. He did not seem to want to stay unless He was needed and wanted. But the disciples **constrained** Jesus, and not only did He stay, but He also sat and ate with them.

How then can a wife learn to constrain her husband? Allow me to use the life of Lydia to draw some conclusions about this.

① **The outward appearance of a woman can give her constraining power.** As a seller of purple, I believe that Lydia was a lovely lady outwardly. She recognized beauty, and she shared it with others. A lovely outward appearance is important to a man, and it has much constraining power. I myself would rather spend time with a person who is clean and neat than with one who is unkempt and sloppy. However, outward appearance can only go so far in constraining a man. I have heard of men who were repulsed by the presence of their beautiful wives, enough to avoid them or even to divorce them. There must be something more that a woman needs in order to constrain a man.

② **The character of a woman can give her constraining power.** I have no doubt that Lydia was a hard-working, industrious woman as she sold her fabric. A beautiful woman loses her constraining power with her husband when he finds that her beauty is only skin deep. Beauty alone will not cause a woman to keep a clean house, to cook consistently good meals, to stay caught up on the laundry or to train godly children. There is something about a woman with character which draws her family to her even after her outward beauty has begun to fade.

③ **The worship of a woman can give her constraining power.** The Bible tells us that Lydia worshiped God even before she was saved. One of my favorite Bible statements is Psalm 96:9a which says, *"O worship the LORD in the beauty of holiness."*

There is a special beauty which the woman who worships the Lord possesses. Her outward beauty will fade and her character can be downright irritating and abrasive, but there is something compelling about a woman who worships the Lord, not in a pious or hypocritical way, but in a humble and sincere way. The woman who worships the Lord possesses a peace and a consistency which makes her compelling to be around. Lydia used her spirituality to constrain Paul by saying, *"...If ye have judged me to be faithful to the Lord, come into my house, and abide there...."*

A wife is commanded in Ephesians to worship or to reverence her own husband. The respect and admiration which a man receives from his wife does not cause him to take her for granted or to walk all over her. Rather it causes him to want to come home from work early so that he can spend more time with her. It causes him to seek her comfort when no one else seems to care, much less worship him.

④ **The hospitality of a woman can give her constraining power.** Lydia provided a place for Paul and those with him to abide for a while. A woman should make her home a lovely place to be so that her husband and children feel constrained to be there. No one wants to come home to a messy, filthy place. I am afraid that many men work late and many children choose their friend's house after school because they are fleeing the disorganization of their own home.

It does not have to cost a lot to make a home pretty, and it doesn't cost anything to be clean. If you have not been taught how to be clean, swallow your pride and ask someone to teach you. If you have been taught, continue to learn. I have read many books about how to clean and organize a home, and I still have much I need to learn.

⑤ **The need of a woman can give her constraining power.** The prettiest of homes is not compelling if the woman who lives there does not convince her family that they are wanted and needed there. Lydia **sought** for Paul. I believe she sought him because she wanted him to give her more instruction about her new-found salvation. She convinced him that she needed his help. If she had not sought him and urged him to come, he would not have come.

A woman's desire for her man is her most compelling quality. Modern women have told their husbands that "anything you can do, I can do better." Because of this, husbands consider their role in the home to be an unneeded one; and husbands and fathers are either uninvolved or absent from the home.

If a man feels that the woman he loves really desires his help, he will lasso the moon if she asks him. Because of this, it is important that a woman first learn to be spiritual before she learns to be a compelling wife. Unspiritual wives may use their wiles to constrain their husbands to do the wrong things.

Mothers should teach their daughters to build their spiritual lives and their walk with God **before** they begin to date. Too many girls begin compelling guys to ask them for dates before they establish a spiritual walk and character which will make them worthy to use such power.

A woman who walks with the Lord must realize that feminine appeal is not a bad attribute to possess. In fact, it can be very good. It can influence an entire household to be saved and to live for the Lord as Lydia's constraining power did.

6 **The love of a woman can give her constraining power.** The Bible says in II Corinthians 5:14a, "*For the love of Christ constraineth us.*" Jesus is the most compelling One of all. He could compel us by force, but He chooses instead to compel us by His love. A mother who compels her children by force will only influence them while they are young enough to fear her; a mother who compels her children by love will always have proper influence over them.

My prayer is that each of us would be filled with the compelling love of Christ, so much so that those we love are drawn to our presence. It is then that we can influence them to be what God would have them to be.

The Preacher's Wife

A Lesson From Priscilla

"*Her children arise up, and call her blessed;
her husband also, and he praiseth her…
and let her own works praise her in the gates.*"
(Proverbs 31:28, 31b)

Chapter 22
Priscilla
Acts 18:24-28; Romans 16:3;
I Corinthians 16:19

*P*RISCILLA AND HER husband Aquila had a church which met in their house. This leads me to believe that Priscilla was a pastor's wife. I know that Priscilla and Aquila, during some time of their life, worked as tentmakers. Perhaps someone other than her husband led the flock which met in her house, but regardless, I think we can learn some things from Priscilla about being the first lady of the church or about being the wife of a preacher.

(1) **Priscilla knew the Word of God and the way of the Lord along with her husband.** The Bible tells us that Priscilla and Aquila expounded the Word of God to a certain preacher named Apollos. I have heard preachers' wives admonished not to follow on the coat strings of their husbands' spirituality, and I know that this is good advice. The pastor's wife should have her own personal walk with the Lord.

Though I do not wish to use myself as the best example, I have spent many hours reading, memorizing and studying the Word of God. Why? Because I want to know the Word of God. I enjoy hearing both my husband and my father preach. They have taught me a lot about the Word of God through their preaching. But I am not satisfied with knowing the Bible just in this way. I want to discover the Bible in a personal way.

Let me say that it is not masculine for a lady to be a student of the Bible. A wife should not flaunt her knowledge before her husband, but the more Bible knowledge a woman has, the more wisdom she can develop so that she can help her husband in his ministry. Many women are great hindrances to their husbands, to the men of God, and to their local church. Why? Because they have no knowledge of how to live the Christian life. They have not searched the Scriptures in order to learn how they can get along with other church members and so forth.

I am sure that I have hindered my husband at some time in his ministry. Without my relationship with the Bible, I know that I could not have been what help to my husband that the Lord has allowed me to be.

The primary reason for my having written two books about Bible women is that I want today's woman to realize how much is in the Bible, not just for men who are called into the ministry, but also for women—for the common, everyday housewives. I hope these chapters have opened your eyes, if they had not been opened already, to that fact. Sometimes people say to me that they cannot believe what I can find in just a few Bible verses. I appreciate the compliment, but may I explain to you why I find such treasures. I find them because I search for them, and I have been searching for a long time.

(2) **Priscilla took the time to explain the way of the Lord and to entertain the man of God along with her husband.** Priscilla was her husband's partner not only in the tentmaking business, but also in ministry, which is what I believe God intended every woman to be. I don't think that a woman can be involved in her husband's ministry to the same extent that he is. The home and the children should play a more vital role in her life. But a woman should seek her husband's advice, and find a way to be involved in what her husband does for the Lord.

There are three methods I find that Priscilla used to help her husband in his ministry.

A. *Priscilla used hospitality.* She opened her home to men of God such as Paul and Apollos, and she opened her home to her husband's flock. Inviting people into the home, not permanently, but occasionally, is a good way for a woman to be involved in her husband's ministry. Housing and feeding pastors and missionaries is a great way to help in the ministry. By doing this, a wife can be helping her husband, and at the same time, she can be nurturing and training her children in the home. What better lesson for children to learn than how to serve the servants of God?

B. *Priscilla used counsel.* She and Aquila counseled Apollos in the way of the Lord. Some of my sweetest memories of the ministry my husband and I share are the times we have been used to counsel people, particularly in marital counseling. I do not seek people to counsel. Actually, I must confess that I sometimes try to avoid it. But when opportunity arises for a pastor's wife to counsel, it is then that she will be grateful if she has been seeking knowledge from the Word of God.

I do not give my husband counsel unless he asks for it, and there are certain areas where I probably would not give him counsel even if he asked. His preaching is an example of one of those areas. I do believe there have been times when our counsel to each other has played a vital role in our lives. I do not believe we both would have continued on in God's will if we had not been wise in our counsel to each other through these years.

I still lack wisdom, but I am glad that I have been storing up knowledge from the Bible these many years. Wisdom says in Proverbs 8:17, "*I love them that love me; and those that seek me early shall find me.*" I began seeking God's counsel on a fairly consistent basis when I was eight years old.

A pastor's wife cannot find wisdom today for the problems she will encounter with people today. She is to be storing up that wisdom day after day. Then the proper counsel will be readily available when she needs to use it.

A pastor's wife who does not seek wisdom from the Bible will be more easily swayed by the world's philosophies. If she is not careful, her counsel will be more humanistic and liberal in content than it is Biblical. We should not seek our wisdom from the latest talk show, secular book, or magazine. I am not saying that these are always wrong, but they usually are. It often startles me to find humanistic thinking among the Christians I encounter across the country. Why is there such thinking among Christian women? I believe we have been lazy in our approach to studying God's Word...or perhaps, even too busy.

C. *Priscilla used service to the man of God.* In Romans 16:3, Paul calls Priscilla and Aquila his helpers in Christ. Not only did Priscilla entertain Paul and Apollos in their home, but Paul worked with Priscilla and Aquila for a while as a tentmaker.

I have found that pastors' wives and deacons' wives are sometimes known as the troublemakers in the church. What a hindrance this is to their husbands and to their work for the Lord! A preacher's wife can be a great help rather than a hindrance to her husband by praying for and honoring those men with whom her husband labors. The wife who exalts the man of God before her children and before her husband nurtures their spiritual lives in an immeasurable way.

(3) **Priscilla was patient with the weaknesses of others.** Priscilla did not dismiss the preacher, Apollos, as ignorant when she heard him teaching the Word incorrectly. Priscilla realized that preachers are human and they sometimes make mistakes. Priscilla's knowledge of the Bible, in this instance, was greater than the preacher's. Did this cause Priscilla to become disenchanted with preachers or to become a troublemaker? No, instead she served, honored and helped the men of God.

(4) **Priscilla was respected and honored by God's man.** Paul took the time to salute Priscilla and Aquila in his second letter to Timothy. (II Timothy 4:19) The word *salute* means "to greet with respect and honor." A pastor's wife should be the most respected lady in the church. For many years my pastor's wife was my mother. I know she is very respected among the folks in our church, as well as among the men of God who know her.

However, a pastor's wife should not seek respect and honor for herself. Instead, she should study God's Word so that she will be ready at any time to help her husband and his people. She should be a servant to God's people, especially to God's men and to her husband. In doing so, *"Her children arise up and call her blessed; her husband also, and he praiseth her…and let her own works praise her in the gates."* (Proverbs 31:28, 31b)

Passing Our Faith Along

A Lesson From Lois and Eunice

"When I call to remembrance the unfeigned faith that is in thee, which dwelt first in thy grandmother Lois, and thy mother Eunice; and I am persuaded that in thee also."
(II Timothy 1:5)

Chapter 23
Lois and Eunice
11 Timothy 1:5

"When I call to remembrance the unfeigned faith that is in thee, which dwelt first in thy grandmother Lois, and thy mother Eunice; and I am persuaded that in thee also." (II Timothy 1:5)

WHEN I WAS in junior high school, I began to question God. I questioned whether He answered my prayers and whether His Word was true. I questioned whether He was even there at all. And then I remembered my grandmother's spirit....

My grandmother, Coystal Mattie Hyles, lost her mother when she was the tender age of eight years old. She became the chief housekeeper, cook, and laundress at this young age, and I suppose in many ways, she left her childhood behind her. Mamaw, as I called her, married very young. Two of her children went to Heaven at the age of seven. Because of the consequences of the Great Depression, my grandfather lost his business and became an alcoholic. He beat my grandmother and finally left her when my father was in junior high. My grandmother reared my father alone and in poverty. But my grandmother had a happy spirit....

When I entered this world, Mamaw was already an old and wrinkled lady. I sat on her lap one day, as a very little child, and asked her why her skin looked like a prune. She took that statement very good-naturedly and often teased me about it. I never knew my grandmother to be a very beautiful woman on the outside. She was a woman small in stature, but she had a very, very large spirit....

I spent many nights at my grandmother's little apartment. I sought refuge in that little apartment many a time, as my father did, when things were going wrong during my high school and college years. I loved my mamaw deeply and felt very close to her. I knew that she loved me. She told me with her spirit....

When Mamaw died, she was almost 97. I was twenty-five, a young wife with a handsome husband, a three-year-old daughter and another baby on the way. Mamaw died two months before my son was born. I gave my son the middle name of "Frasure," which was my grandmother's maiden name. By the time my grandmother died, she could not see nor could she walk very well. Humanly speaking, she had very little to offer me, but I missed her deeply...I missed her spirit.

It was that spirit which quickly answered my questioning as a junior high girl. I remember being alone in my bedroom and thinking of my grandmother. I thought of all she had been through and of how old she was. (Of course, to me she already seemed ancient!) I thought of her happy spirit. I realized that no woman could be as happy as my grandmother was, in spite of what she had been through, unless she knew Someone Who was greater than she. My grandmother settled my questions—without saying a word. Through her spirit, she persuaded me and she passed on to me her unfeigned faith. Without that spirit, who knows how long I would have questioned or what would have been the answers I found!

My mother, Beverly Joyce Hyles, is a beautiful woman. She is a very talented woman, and though she was tempted to give her talent to the world, she submitted to do whatever God wanted her to do with her life. That has been her desire ever since. That has been her spirit....

My mother is a very humble woman. If you asked her, she would say that she is not a good wife or mother. But I would tell you differently. My mother grew spiritually before my eyes as I was growing up in her home. And if, in the process of growing, she felt she had made a mistake, she would humbly come into my bedroom to apologize and to ask forgiveness. I guess of all the things my mother did which influenced me when I was growing up, that influenced me the most. She had a humble spirit—a meek spirit.

My mother is a quiet person. She married a man who influenced thousands. She prefers privacy. She married a man who was an orator. She is an excellent speaker but would rather not be in front of people. She is lovely and talented, and she could have made quite a name for herself. Instead, she put her family first. She has a quiet spirit....

My mother has endured some difficult battles and trials during her life. Her toughness during these trials has been her greatest lesson to me. Through her spirit, she has passed on to me her unfeigned faith—the unfeigned faith which dwelt first in Lois, then in Eunice, and then in Timothy.

I have much for which to be thankful. I have a grandmother in Heaven and a mother here on this earth who have passed on to me their faith.

I want so badly so serve the Lord. However, I am in a stage of life where I often feel compelled to stay at home and to train my children. I struggle with the many pulls of the ministry. I often question my decisions. "Lord, am I doing the right thing when I say 'no' to others in order to be with my children while they are with me?"

Each time He sweetly confirms my decisions which have been made carefully through my husband's counsel. Each time God reminds me of the value of the life of a mother—a life spent passing on the faith to "little people." A mother is the CEO of the smallest unit of people God ever established. She often feels unimportant...but she isn't.

When mothers possessed meek and quiet spirits, America was a noble and a spiritual country. When mothers began to be proud and bold and to demand their rights, then the whole world seemed to fall apart.

I close this book by saying thank you to God for my grandmother and mother who passed on their unfeigned (sincere) faith to me. They didn't so much do it through words. Rather, they did it through their spirits—their meek and quiet spirits.

And I have made a commitment to pass the faith on to my own two children. What they do with it is up to them. But I shall not devalue the importance of giving it to them. I shall treasure this job more highly than any successful career or lucrative position. I shall esteem it as a high calling of ministry. And I shall strive to do it, not so much with my words; rather, I shall do it through my spirit.

"Lord, Give us a meek and quiet spirit! Amen."

"Likewise, ye wives, be in subjection to your own husbands; that, if any obey not the word, they also may without the word be won by the conversation of the wives;

While they behold your chaste conversation coupled with fear.

Whose adorning let it not be that outward adorning of plaiting the hair, and of wearing of gold, or of putting on of apparel;

But let it be the hidden man of the heart, in that which is not corruptible, even the ornament of a meek and quiet spirit, which is in the sight of God of great price." (I Peter 3:1-4)